►►► **Interpretationshilfen**

Romeo and Juliet

William Shakespeare

Alexandra Dube

D1668248

Cornelsen

Alan Pulverness

Romeo and Juliet · Interpretationshilfe

Verlagsredaktion
Neil Porter

Umschlagdesign
Klein & Halm Grafikdesign, Berlin

Layout & technische Umsetzung
Anna Bakalović und Annika Preyhs, Berlin

Bildquellen: S. 5: National Portrait Gallery, London; © akg-images; S. 7: © British Library, London, UK / The Bridgeman Art Library; S. 12: © picture-alliance/ KPA/HIP/The British Library; S. 20: © Mirisch-7 Arts/United Artists/The Kobal Collection; S. 21: © Cinetext Bildarchiv; S. 24, 26, 28, 33, 35, 39, 45: Romeo and Juliet (1968), © Paramount/The Kobal Collection; S. 31: *Romeo and Juliet* (1936), © Cinetext Bildarchiv; S. 38, 46: *Romeo and Juliet* (1968), © picture-alliance/KPA; S. 48: Wolfgang Mattern, Bochum; S. 49: 'Portrait of a Young Man' by Lorenzo Lotto, © Galleria degli Uffizi, Florence, Italy/The Bridgeman Art Library; S. 55: 'Portrait of Giovanna Tournabuoni' by Domenico Ghirlandaio, © Tokyo Fuji Art Museum, Tokyo, Japan/The Bridgeman Art Library; S. 60: 'Ludovico Sforza' after Leonardo da Vinci, © ullstein bild/Granger Collection; S. 63: 'Anna Selbdritt' by Albrecht Dürer, © Altmann Collection, Metropolitan Museum of Art, New York/akg-images/Erich Lessing; S. 64: 'Portrait of a Franciscan Monk' by Peter Paul Rubens, © Galleria Doria Pamphilj, Rome, Italy/Alinari/The Bridgeman Art Library

www.cornelsen.de

1. Auflage, 1. Druck 2007

© 2007 Cornelsen Verlag, Berlin

Druck: CS-Druck CornelsenStürtz, Berlin

ISBN 978-3-589-22433-3

 Inhalt gedruckt auf säurefreiem Papier aus nachhaltiger Forstwirtschaft.

Contents

William Shakespeare 5

Historical Background 7

    Shakespeare's Theatre 7

    Women and Families
    in Shakespeare's Time 10

    The Four Humours 12

Sources 15

Reception 17

The Story 22

Characters 47

Themes 68

Language and Style 80

Glossary of Literary Terms 89

Coping with Exam Papers 91

Written Test 95

All page and line references are to the Cornelsen edition of *Romeo and Juliet* (Berlin: Cornelsen Verlag, 2007) ISBN 978-3-06-031206-1.

When citing lines of poetry in this book, we have cited them as if they were prose. For example, Romeo says on first seeing Juliet:

> It seems she hangs upon the cheek of night
> Like the rich jewel in an Ethiop's ear.
> (I, v, 44–45)

The correct way of citing these lines would be to include a slash where the line of poetry ends: '*It seems she hangs upon the cheek of night / Like the rich jewel in an Ethiop's ear*'. We, however, have cited the lines in the following way: '*It seems she hangs upon the cheek of night like the rich jewel in an Ethiop's ear*' (I, v, 44–45), in order to bring out the meaning of the sentence. Your teacher will advise you how he or she would like you to cite lines from the play.

William Shakespeare

Surprisingly little is known about William Shakespeare, considering he that is probably the most famous playwright who ever lived.

He was born in Stratford-upon-Avon in April 1564. He married Anne Hathaway in 1582, with whom he had three children, Susanna, Hamnet and Judith. Little else is known about him until 1592, when Shakespeare is mentioned as being a playwright. It is also known that he worked as an actor and that he was part-owner of a playing company (a company of actors) called 'The Lord Chamberlain's Men'. In 1603 King James took over the patronage of the company and it was renamed 'The King's Men'. Shakespeare became a wealthy man and bought properties in London and Stratford. He retired to Stratford in around 1614 and died there on 23 April 1616.

During his lifetime he wrote 37 plays. He may have written more but these have not survived. Although 18 of his plays were published during his lifetime, most of these editions (called 'quartos') were probably not overseen by Shakespeare. Their texts may have been reconstructed from memory by a member or members of the cast of the plays.

It was only in 1623 that his plays were first published together in what is called 'The First Folio'. But as Shakespeare was by then dead, it cannot be said that the First Folio is a definitive text. However, it was the first time that many of his plays were printed.

Shakespeare is unusual in that he wrote a wide variety of plays. Not only did he write history plays that covered over a hundred years of English history, he was also equally competent at tragedy (e.g. *Hamlet*) as well as comedy (e.g. *Much Ado about Nothing*).

Besides being a playwright, he was also a prolific poet: he wrote a cycle of 154 sonnets as well as several long poems.

Shakespeare's reputation grew slowly after his death. By the end of the 20th century he had become the most performed dramatist in the world. Many of the lines from his plays and poems are still well-known today.

Historical Background ◄◄◄

Shakespeare's Theatre

To understand how Shakespeare's plays first appeared to an audience, one needs to recognize the importance of the place in which they were first performed and the role played by the audience. The theatres (the Curtain and later the Globe) were basically round buildings ('this wooden O', as the theatre is called in the Prologue to *Henry V*) that had developed only recently from the courtyards of inns where plays had previously been performed, and were still open to the sky. The plays were performed during the day

The Globe Theatre

so that both performers and audience were similarly lit. Our modern theatres with silent audiences watching a lit space from the dark would be incomprehensible to an Elizabethan audience, who were encouraged to participate. Indeed, it may well be helpful to consider the stage at this period not just as a place to watch a story unfold, but also as an arena where swordplay and wordplay were both cheered along by the spectators. The audience in Shakespeare's day had no idea of going along with the fiction of the theatre – what the 19th-century Romantic poet Coleridge called a 'willing suspension of disbelief': they were constantly aware that they were watching a play.

The stage itself, relatively small (about 14 metres across and about 9 metres deep) and projecting out into the audience, was called an 'apron' stage and was about a metre above the ground, so the audience could feel they were part of the action. The richer members of the audience were seated either on the stage or in three tiered galleries, protected from the weather by a thatched roof, while the rest of the audience watched the performance standing in the area around and in front of the stage, and were thus known as the 'groundlings'. If it rained, both actors and groundlings got wet, and this is also true at the reconstructed Globe Theatre in London today.

Above the main acting area was an overhanging balcony, which could represent the battlements of a castle or a bedroom window, such as Juliet's. (There is no actual mention of a balcony in *Romeo and Juliet*, although Act II, Scene 2, in which Romeo appears beneath Juliet's window, is conventionally known as 'the balcony scene' because her window has usually been presented as a balcony on stage.) The actors' entrances and exits were made either from doors at the back of the stage, or from a curtained area below the balcony, or – for sudden appearances and disappearances – through a trapdoor in the floor. In Act IV, Scene 5 we see the use of the curtained area, when the Nurse discovers Juliet's body; Act V, Scene 3 also makes use of the different areas of the stage, as it is clear that the vault where Juliet lies is separate from other areas where the action takes place. Scenery was minimal and there were few props, as there was nowhere to store them and no wings in which to hide them from the audience.

Costumes were generally quite elaborate, though always contemporary, so that *Romeo and Juliet*, though set in Verona, would have been performed in 16th-century English dress. The life enacted on stage would have been instantly recognizable to the audience. When the Capulet servants make puns on the word 'coal' in the opening scene of the play, when they complain about cleaning the dishes ('*scrape a trencher*'; I, v, 2), or when Lord Capulet orders the Servant to fetch drier logs (IV, iv, 16), these are direct reflections of English domestic life of the time.

With little scenery and few props, the audience needed the dialogue to tell them where they were. We learn, for example, from the Chorus that the play is set in Verona. We know that Juliet is living in a house that is well protected, as Benvolio points out the orchard wall (II, i, 5) and Juliet later reminds the audience: '*The orchard walls are high and hard to climb*' (II, ii, 63). As the action of Shakespeare's plays was originally continuous – the scenes and stage directions were added later by editors – it is common for characters to tell the audience where the next scene is going to take place: '*Hence will I to my ghostly friar's close cell*' (II, ii, 188); '*Hie you to church; [...] hie you to the cell*' (II, v, 72, 77).

The Elizabethan dramatist also used the language of the play to tell the audience what time of day it was – day or night – and who the characters were. In Act III, Scene 1, Benevolio tells us '*The day is hot*' (III, i, 2). In Act V, Scene 3 Paris sets the scene and tells the audience it is night by describing the yew tree in the churchyard and asking the Page for the torch.

Scenes could not open with a large number of characters on stage, as the audience would not know who they all were. This explains why so many scenes begin with two or three characters talking, who are then joined by others who are named as they arrive. We know who Romeo is when he comes on stage for the first time (I, i, 148) due to his parents' and Benvolio's conversation about him, which takes place just beforehand. In another instance the audience is prepared for the crowd at the Capulets' feast in Act I, Scenes 5 and 6 through the device of Romeo reading out the list of invited guests in Act I, Scene 2.

Without sets and lighting, exits, too, were problematic, and this is one explanation for so many deaths – such as that of Mercutio – taking place offstage. Otherwise it would have been difficult to have their bodies removed from stage. This convention does actually make the onstage deaths of Romeo and Juliet more striking by contrast.

We know little about the styles of performance in Shakespeare's theatre, apart from the fact that women were not allowed to perform in the theatre, so all the female roles in Shakespeare's plays would have been played by young male actors. This sometimes allows for moments of humour shared between cast and audience. When Mercutio says of the Nurse that she needs her fan '*to hide her face; for her fan's the fairer face*' (II, iv, 99–100), this was perhaps a line designed to amuse the groundlings, who would have been close enough to see the Nurse's (male) face.

In some of Shakespeare's plays there are plays within the plays (e.g. in *Hamlet* and *A Midsummer Night's Dream*) which give us some idea of the style of performance. But we can only speculate about matters such as the pace of the productions and whether the acting was realistic or melodramatic. Given the conditions in the theatre, with the audience moving around and responding vocally to the action on stage, it is likely that the actors would have had to deliver their lines in loud voices with very clear enunciation. The texts themselves offer us some clues to their author's probable intentions, though not necessarily to the actors' interpretations.

Women and Families in Shakespeare's Time

Women had a very different status in Elizabethan England from their social identity today. Despite the fact that the nation was ruled by a queen, Queen Elizabeth I, who was a strong- and independent-minded woman, women were seen as being the property of their husbands. When Capulet talks to Paris about Juliet, he describes her as one of several '*fennel buds*' (I, ii, 29) and this image of young women as existing to be picked demonstrates his view of women as a commodity. Some social historians consider that the Protestantism that developed after Henry VIII split from the Catholic Church was detrimental to women, as their only role in society was that of wife. Previously women had been able to exercise power within convents, free from male interference. The new attitude of submission by women can be seen in the Protestant *Book of Common Prayer*, first published in 1549. The priest is directed to read to a newly married couple St. Paul's letter to the Ephesians, in which he instructs women to submit to their husbands: 'as the Church in congregation is subject unto Christ: so likewise let the wives be in subjection unto their own husbands in all things.' Capulet may speak of Juliet as the object of all his hopes (I, ii, 15), but he will throw her out of his house (III, v) if she dares to disobey him. His attitude also reflects the position of children within the family. It was a common practice for children of all ages to kneel and ask for their parents' blessing each time they entered and left the house.

Yet a woman could inherit property if her husband died and if there were no sons. The eldest son inherited first, which meant that a younger son needed a better education or to marry a woman with property. Inheritance was central to the security and, in many cases, survival of a family. Yet in several of Shakespeare's plays (for example, *Othello* and *A Midsummer Night's Dream*, as well as *Romeo and Juliet*) the central characters place love on a higher level than duty to family, a reminder that literature is not generally intended to be an accurate reflection of life.

The family itself was also different from the family in today's Western society, being based on a wider kinship network. The importance of maintaining and ensuring the continuation of the household was at the heart of English land-owning society and it was thus essential to have heirs to inherit land and property. There are several reported instances from this period of what we would consider to be horrific brutality against girls who refused to marry the men chosen by their parents. The tragedy for the parents of Romeo and Juliet is not simply the loss of their children – the death of children was common as noted by the Nurse (I, iii, 21–22) – but the death of their last remaining children, and thus their heirs. The need to sustain his household – which includes dependents and servants – is what drives Capulet. Paris is a kinsman of the Prince and a suitable suitor for Juliet for economic reasons (although Romeo would have been equally acceptable from a social and financial perspective). Capulet is portrayed as a man who enjoys his position and wealth – he takes over the organization of the kitchen to ensure that the banquet will be suitably impressive for his guests. He rages against his daughter when she refuses to marry Paris, and thus challenges his authority and threatens to undermine the control he exerts over his household. To escape her father's wishes, Juliet could choose to become a nun or to die.

Although it was customary at this time to think that marriage for affection or romantic reasons was foolish if not immoral, Shakespeare in *Romeo and Juliet* elevates and celebrates the love between the two young people, changing the moral of his play from his source material, which had condemned the relationship. He invites the audience to take the part of the lovers against family pressure and social custom. The theme of children outwitting their parents was widespread, existing in folklore and legend, and it is one to which Shakespeare returns several times in his plays. But whereas in most versions of this theme, the children's struggle is against misguided parents or evil step-parents, in *Romeo and Juliet*, the parents, although feuding with each other, are shown to care deeply about their children. Capulet's anger against Juliet would not have been considered excessive at the time, and his decision to marry her swiftly to Paris is to help her overcome her grief over the death of Tybalt would have been understood in a positive light. Thus the audience is not given a simplistic view of the stereotypical battle between parent and child, but a much more subtle depiction of both sides of the conflict.

The Four Humours

In Shakespeare's day people believed that the universe was made up of four elements – earth, water, fire and air – and that the human body was similarly made up of four humours. These were: blood, phlegm, black bile and yellow bile. These bodily fluids determined the physical complexion of a person, as well as their temperament:

Blood was linked with air and created a sanguine personality, someone who was happy and generous. Blood was considered hot and moist.

Phlegm was linked with water and produced a phlegmatic person, who was pale and calm but cowardly. Phlegm was associated with cold and moist.

A human being was viewed as having a mixture of the four humours.

Black bile was linked with the earth and created a melancholic person, who was creative and sentimental but also lazy. Black bile was considered cold and dry.

Yellow bile was linked with fire and produced a choleric personality, who was angry, energetic and also violent. Yellow bile was viewed as hot and dry.

The perfect temperament was thought to be an even blend of all four humours. In *Julius Caesar*, for example,

Mark Antony says of Brutus: 'His life was gentle, and the elements so mixed in him that Nature might stand up and say to all the world, "This was a man!"' In *Romeo and Juliet*, the Friar tells Romeo that getting up at dawn demonstrates '*a distempered head*' (II, iii, 33), a head in which the humours are not properly balanced.

In addition to balance, heat was considered to be more important than cold and was thought to be a masculine characteristic. Interestingly, in this play, Romeo is shown to be melancholy and romantic, an unlucky and '*fearful man*' (III, iii, 1), but he is 'heated' by the passion of Juliet who is described as 'hot' by the Nurse and others. When Lady Capulet says '*You are too hot*' (III, v, 175), critics are divided as to whether she is addressing her angry husband or her wilful daughter. Twice in the play we are told that Juliet was born on 'Lammas-eve', which traditionally meant that she was ruled by Leo. Astrology was at this time considered as a science, and Shakespeare's audience would have associated Leo with people who were choleric and passionate. The sign was also linked with youth, summer and the sun. Romeo calls Juliet '*the sun*' (II, ii, 3) and says she teaches '*the torches to burn bright!*' (I, v, 43), while the Prince after her death declares that: '*The sun, for sorrow, will not show his head*' (V, iii, 306).

The theory of the four humours had been the basis of medicine since medieval times, and Shakespeare's audience would have been able to read the signs in his plays and identify which of his characters demonstrated which 'humour'. The play also distributes the four humours evenly between the minor characters to create a balance of mood in each scene. Thus the choleric, angry Tybalt contrasts with the easy-going and phlegmatic Benvolio, and the choleric Lord Capulet with the phlegmatic Nurse. Juliet notes that many old people appear to have a phlegmatic nature as they are '*Unwieldy, slow, heavy and pale as lead*' (II, v, 17).

▶ **Revision**
(what you learn in this section)
- Drama and theatre were relatively new developments in England.
- Staging a play was not easy, as there were many limitations: lighting was a problem, there was little scenery and there were few props, women were not allowed to act, the audience could be disruptive.

- Shakespeare used his actors to explain what the setting was, what time of day it was and who the characters were.
- Women had a lower status than men, and were seen as being the property of their husbands, just as their children were seen as his property too.
- Marriage was rarely seen as a result of love; rather it was used a means of gaining status, property and money.
- It was believed that a person was made up of the four elements, which would influence his or her character. Astrology was also popular.

Sources

The tale of two lovers who fall in love despite the hatred between their two families and who die together rather than live apart is an ancient story. There were many different and popular versions of it in 15th-century Europe, particularly in Italy.

The poet Arthur Brooke used three Italian stories to create a narrative poem called 'The Tragicall Historye of Romeus and Juliet'. This poem, written in 1562, was Shakespeare's primary source, though he also knew a later prose version of the story by William Painter. It is considered likely that he had also read or seen performed in the theatre an English translation of a play called *A Story Newly Found of Two Noble Lovers*. This was based on a work by Luigi Da Porto, published around 1530 (which also inspired Brooke). The Da Porto narrative is important as it for the first time sets the action in Verona, gives the lovers the names Romeo and Giulietta, the two feuding families the surnames Montecchi and Cappelletti. Da Porto also describes Romeo going disguised to a carnival ball at his enemy's house in the hope of seeing a lady who scorns his love, just as Shakespeare's Romeo does in the hope of seeing Rosaline.

The idea that stories should be totally original is a modern concept, and in Elizabethan times a writer was judged by the way in which he adapted and shaped existing texts. In the case of the Brooke poem one of the major changes was with regard to time. In the poem, the story takes nine months to unfold, while Shakespeare compresses it into four days. This creates a sense of urgency and the feeling that the lovers have no means of escape (cf. 'Time', p. 73).

Shakespeare also changes Juliet's age: in Brooke's poem she is 16, in the play not quite 14. But most significantly, he also changes the narrative attitude towards the lovers. Brooke's poem has a strict moral tone, announced in his Preface which refers to 'unhonest desire', 'neglect of authority and parental advice' and 'shame of stolen contracts'. He clearly takes the side of the parents and demonstrates how the lovers' disobedience leads to disaster. Shakespeare, on the other hand, through the characterization of Romeo and Juliet, enables the audience to identify with them. In Shakespeare's play the older generation are shown to be disobedient to the rules of society through their family feud, and this '*ancient grudge*' creates the unforgiving code of honour which leads to the death of the lovers.

Shakespeare's play has become so popular worldwide that it has eclipsed its sources. Verona now promotes itself as the city of Romeo and Juliet. Tourist brochures and websites invite visitors to see the 'real' home of Juliet's family, with the balcony where the lovers exchanged their vows (which was actually added to the medieval house in the 1930s) and 'Juliet's tomb', a popular place for local wedding couples to pose for photographs. It is true that there was the ancient Italian family of Cappelletti in Italy (in Cremona) who had a notorious feud with a family in Verona called Montecchi, but there is no history of their having any children named Romeo or Juliet, or of an illicit romantic liaison between the two families. The Verona tourist industry, however, has benefited from the myth for several centuries. Today over 5000 letters are sent to Verona from around the world asking Juliet for advice (inspiring the 1993 song cycle 'The Juliet Letters' by Elvis Costello and the Brodsky Quartet), which demonstrates the desire of contemporary audiences for realism surrounding fictional texts.

There is one more additional source for the poetry of the play – Petrarch. The love poetry of the Italian poet Petrarch (1304–1374) was extremely popular in Elizabethan England and the images found in his poetry are the source for the courtly love language used by Romeo and mocked by Mercutio, who lists the names of the heroines celebrated by the poet (II, iv, 38–43).

Reception

A Note on the Text

It is generally presumed that *Romeo and Juliet* was first performed in ca. 1594, so it is one of Shakespeare's earlier plays. Whichever version you are reading cannot be seen as the one 'true' version, as the play was compiled from a variety of sources. The first version (published in Quarto form, a particular way of printing and cutting paper), known as Q1 and published in 1597, has been frequently described as 'the bad Quarto' by editors, since it was presumably put together by some of the actors who appeared in an early production of the play and is lacking important scenes and contains many inaccuracies. This first published edition had the title 'An Excellent conceited Tragedie of Romeo and Juliet, As it hath been often (with great applause) played publicly'. Its popularity would have been one reason for a publisher to have the play printed (copyright as we know it did not exist then).

The second version (Q2, published in 1599) is thought to have been printed from Shakespeare's rough notes; the important anthology of Shakespeare's plays published in 1623 (the First Folio) uses this as its basis. This edition stated that it was 'newly corrected, augmented, and amended as it hath been sundry times publicly acted'. Contemporary versions mostly follow Q2. Thus you may find many words are different in different editions of the play. Equally, when you see a production of the play, you will find different parts are cut, depending on what the director wants to highlight in his or her version. A play is essentially a production, and the text is just a blueprint for a stage performance. More than anyone, Shakespeare was aware of this.

The History of *Romeo and Juliet*'s Performance

Romeo and Juliet is one of the most popular plays ever written, and it has remained in production almost constantly since the 16th century. This is a play which has been reinterpreted and rewritten for different ages. It is a play which, as the famous director Peter Brook has noted, belongs to each age in the manner in which it is performed.

Today when we see the play, it may be advertised – as was the 1996 Baz Lurhmann film *William Shakespeare's Romeo + Juliet* – as 'The greatest love story the world has ever known'. Publicity for this film also included the following promotional slogans:
– The Classic Love Story Set in Our Time
– Hope & Despair. Tragedy & Love. Romeo & Juliet.
– From Age to Age One Classic Story is as Timeless as Love Itself
– My only love sprung from my only hate
Yet contemporary productions may choose to emphasize other features of the play such as the political or social background – the two lovers fighting convention in choosing to love each other, or gender issues, highlighting Juliet's position in her world. Few contemporary productions, however, emphasize the fatalistic theme of the play, although this is still often discussed when the text is analysed and is thought to have been an aspect of the play that Shakespeare's own contemporaries would have appreciated.

Following the restoration of Charles II to the throne of England in 1662, when the theatres were re-opened after being shut by the Puritans, the play was produced by the actor-manager, William Davenant (1606–1668), Shakespeare's godson. He was responsible for most of the 17th-century productions of Shakespeare's plays. However, this was the last production of the play as we know it today for over 70 years. In 1679, Thomas Otway rewrote it as *The History and Fall of Caius Marius*. Otway renamed the lovers Marius and Lavinia and made it a political play set in ancient Rome. *Romeo and Juliet* returned to the stage in 1744, but even this production used many of Otway's changes, including a scene in which Juliet wakes up before Romeo dies.

The first successful production of the play in the 18th century was by the actor David Garrick in 1748. This production, too, was far removed from the original. Garrick wanted a powerful role for himself and a simple melodrama that would please his audience. He therefore retained Otway's final death scene in the tomb between the two lovers and cut out all the bawdy jokes. He also reduced Mercutio's part, as Garrick wanted to be the centre of attention throughout and not have another actor make long speeches while he was on stage. His version of *Romeo and Juliet* became the standard text for the next one hundred years. It was also very popular. Between 1751 and 1800, there were 399 performances of the play in London, more than any other Shakespeare play.

During the 19th century, it was Juliet who became the most important character and the part many of the great actresses of the age wished to play. The fashion during this period was for realism and huge period settings were built for vast crowd scenes. It was not until the beginning of the 20th century that the theatrical manager William Poel, who believed that the most important things were Shakespeare's words and the poetry, removed the clutter and reinstated Shakespeare's text. Some of the most famous productions and performances of the 20th century were those of John Gielgud and Laurence Olivier, including one in which they exchanged the parts of Romeo and Mercutio on alternate nights. During the first part of the 20th century, the focus of productions was on the poetry of the play, but by the second half of the century this emphasis changed and many productions emphasized either the youth/age conflict or saw the lovers as part of a political struggle between the state and feudal families.

The play has inspired many composers such as Bellini, Berlioz, Gounod, Tchaikovsky and Prokofiev, whose ballet music has been widely choreographed. Here *Romeo and Juliet* is a simple love story and most of the sub-text of the play is ignored. The feud itself has also become the focus of many contemporary versions. One of the most successful was Leonard Bernstein's 1957 musical *West Side Story* (lyrics by Stephen Sondheim) which transposed the story to 1950s New York, where the feud was fought out between the street gangs of the Sharks and the Jets. This was filmed in 1961 and has often been revived with different ethnic groups providing the conflict.

The many film versions of the play range from George Cukor's 1936 film which, like the stage productions of the era, concentrated on the poetry of the play, to Franco Zeffirelli's film, made in 1968. This, in tune with the *zeitgeist*, highlighted the theme of youth and love, and is best remembered for its lovingly-shot Italian locations. Baz Luhrmann in 1996 made the lovers into beautiful teenagers in a world of gangsters and, like the Zeffirelli film before it, drew on the pop culture of the day.

Other screen versions have included the thrillers *China Girl* (1987), *Romeo is Bleeding* (1993) and *Romeo Must Die* (2000), the cross-cultural romances *Mississippi Masala* and *Jungle Fever* (both 1991) and the breakdancing movie *Rooftops* (1989). In *Shakespeare in Love* (1998), the playwright Tom Stoppard imagines that the play is inspired by Shakespeare's own love story.

The themes of *Romeo and Juliet* have inspired many plays, novels, films and pop adaptations in which the conflict that separates the lovers covers the globe and even beyond (e.g. the mutants and the normals in the X-men comics and films). The play has also inspired a recent play, *After Juliet* (1999) by Sharman Macdonald, centred on the character of Rosaline and continuing the story after the death of the lovers. The play is written for young people and, according to its

Film Posters for *West Side Story* and *William Shakespeare's Romeo + Juliet*

author, can be staged anywhere: 'This could be Verona. Or it could be Edinburgh, Dublin, New York or Liverpool. It could be 1500, 1900, 2000 or 3000.' The themes of *Romeo and Juliet* are both international and for all times.

Romeo and Juliet has also become a key text for scholars since the beginning of the 20th century to explore gender and imagery in Shakespeare's work, as well as a problematic text in critical debates about the nature of tragedy.

▶▶▶ The Story

Prologue

In an opening sonnet the Chorus informs the audience where the play is set (Verona), but not when it is set. He introduces the long-standing feud between the Montague and Capulet families and summarizes the story that is about to unfold – '*A pair of star-crossed lovers take their life*'.

The outcome of the play is told to the audience.

Close reading: The Prologue

Almost from the first words of the Prologue, we are made aware of the sense of **antithesis** and opposition which will be such central themes in the play – it may be '*fair Verona*', but the beautiful city is disfigured by '*ancient grudge*' which has led to '*new mutiny*'. As with many family feuds that have gone on for a long time, the '*grudge*' is '*ancient*' and probably no one can recall its precise origin, but as we shall see, the often violent antagonism between the two families continues to erupt whenever they meet. The '*civil blood*' that '*makes civil hands unclean*' is the first of many **oxymorons** (combinations of words that would normally be contradictory) throughout the play. 'Civil' has two meanings: a) 'connected with the people who live in a country' (which is where the term 'civil war' derives from); b) 'polite, decent and civilized'. Shakespeare plays with these two meanings to say that the blood of people killed in the strife makes the hands of civilized people unclean.

The Prologue also has another function: ll. 5–11 summarize the whole story of the play. It may seem strange for a playwright to remove any tension by giving away the entire plot in a few opening lines. But in describing Romeo and Juliet as '*A pair of star-crossed lovers*' – lovers hindered by their own destiny – the Prologue actually reinforces the idea of **fatalism**. The audience know from the outset that Romeo and Juliet's love is '*death-marked*', that the lovers will die and that their deaths will '*bury their parents' strife*'. This foreknowledge adds to the feeling of inevitability of fates that are written in the stars; in this way, the play itself becomes a fatal construction from which the lovers cannot escape.

The language of the Prologue further adds to the sense of an inescapable fate beyond the control of human beings. Not only are the lovers '*star-crossed*' – they have come '*from forth the fatal loins*' of the Capulets and Montagues. In other words, their fates were sealed in the womb, before they were even born. Thus the series of '*misadventured piteous overthrows*' – apparently incidental or accidental misfortunes – that lead to the play's tragic outcome (e.g. Friar John's failure to deliver the letter to Romeo) can be seen not as chance or coincidence, but as the workings of fate.

The end of the Prologue returns to the theatrical setting, reminding us that we are watching a play, one that will occupy the stage for (about) two hours. The final two lines are a **rhyming couplet** (two lines that end with the same rhyme; here, '*attend*'/ '*mend*') which assures the audience that the actors will do their best to entertain them.

The Prologue (like the Prologue to Act Two) is in the form of a **sonnet**, a 14-line poem in iambic pentameters (five 'feet' in each line, with each foot consisting of an unstressed syllable followed by a stressed one). The 14 lines are made up of three quatrains (4 lines) followed by a final couplet (2 lines) with the rhyme scheme *abab cdcd efef gg*. There is often a shift in mood or meaning at the beginning of the third quatrain (sometimes called the 'volta' or turning point). In the Prologue, one could divide the quatrains in this way:

1st quatrain (ll. 1–4): An introduction to the feud between the two families.

2nd quatrain (ll. 5–8): The story of the two children from the rival families is told: they fall in love and die.

3rd quatrain: Here, the change ('volta') directs the attention towards the stage ('*Is now the two hours' traffic of our stage*'), but it is noticeable how the verb and subject only occur in the final line of this quatrain. The quatrain begins with '*The fearful passage of their death-marked love*', which serves to intensify the effect of unalterable fate; the next two lines reinforce the depth of the feud while repeating the fact that the lovers will die.

The final couplet continues the reference to the artificiality of the stage and in an almost humble manner ('*shall strive to mend*') hopes that the performance will fill in any details missing in the Prologue.

Rhyming words are often used to emphasize links or contrasts in meaning. In the Prologue some of the rhyming words draw our attention to contrasts or contradictions – '*dignity*'/'*mutiny*'; '*life*'/ '*strife*'; '*love*'/'*remove*' – while others suggest some disturbing connections – '*scene*'/'*unclean*'; '*foes*'/'*overthrows*'.

Act One

Scene 1

In a street in Verona, Sampson and Gregory, two servants of the Capulet household, talk about their family's feud with the Montagues. Sampson boasts of what he will do to the Montague men – and their women. Abraham and Balthasar (two Montague servants) appear, and Sampson makes an insulting gesture at them to provoke a fight. Benvolio (Lord Montague's nephew) appears and

The servants reveal how a feud involves whole households, which include relatives, servants and friends.

'Rebellious subjects, enemies to peace'

separates the servants, but almost immediately, they are joined by Tybalt (Lady Capulet's nephew), who is determined to continue the fight, despite Benvolio's protests that he had only been trying to keep the peace. The fight is joined by '*several of both houses*', including Montague and Capulet, whose wives attempt to stop them from becoming involved, before the Prince (Escales) arrives and commands everyone to stop fighting. This is the third time that a violent brawl has broken out on the streets of Verona, and the Prince warns both families that a further outbreak will be punishable by death.

Benvolio explains to Lord and Lady Montague how the fight escalated. The Montagues are concerned about their son, Romeo, who seems depressed and uncommunicative. Benvolio meets Romeo and quickly discovers the cause of his melancholy: he is infatuated with a beautiful woman who has resisted his advances, swearing to remain chaste for the rest of her life. Benvolio advises Romeo to forget about her and consider other women, but Romeo rejects his friend's advice.

Scene 2

Capulet accepts that it should not be too difficult for old men like him and Montague to keep the peace. He is approached by Paris, a young man who wishes to marry his daughter, Juliet. Capulet points out that Juliet is not yet 14, but if she agrees, he will give his consent. In the meantime, he invites Paris to a banquet that evening, where he says there will be plenty of beautiful women who Paris may find more attractive. Capulet gives a list of guests to a servant, with instructions to seek them out and invite them to the banquet.

> Here we see the first contrast: Benvolio's peacefulness versus Tybalt's aggression.

> Romeo and Rosaline are examples of courtly lovers: he loves her from a distance; she rejects his love.

> Capulet favours the marriage, but he also wants Paris to examine other potential candidates for marriage. Moreover, he implies Juliet must agree to the marriage.

However, the servant is unable to read, and in the street he asks Romeo, who Benvolio is still trying to comfort with thoughts of other women, to read the list for him. The list includes Rosaline (the young woman with whom Romeo is infatuated). Benvolio suggests that Romeo should attend the banquet, to see other, more beautiful women; Romeo is keen to go, but only to see Rosaline.

Here too, it is suggested that Romeo should examine other women.

Scene 3

Lady Capulet and the Nurse reflect on Juliet's age. The Nurse immediately thinks of her own daughter, now dead, who – had she lived – would have been the same age as Juliet. She recalls when Juliet was weaned and how her late husband had joked about Juliet growing up and becoming sexually active. Lady Capulet may disapprove of the Nurse's bawdy humour, or she may simply be irritated by the Nurse's incessant chatter, but she finds it difficult to make her stop. The conversation moves on to the topic of marriage: Lady Capulet tells Juliet she should be thinking about marriage,

'How stands your disposition to be married?'

and mentions the request from Paris, who she praises extravagantly; she uses the metaphor of a book to describe a marriage. Juliet remains non-committal, but agrees to look at him. The guests begin to arrive for the banquet.

Juliet is told that she can decide whether to marry Paris.

Scene 4

Romeo, Benvolio and Mercutio, together with several friends, are on their way to the Capulets' banquet. Romeo is still miserable about his unrequited love for Rosaline, and despite Mercutio's attempts to cheer him up, says he will not dance at the banquet. They put on masks, so as not to be recognized by any of the Capulets. When Romeo refers to a dream he has had, Mercutio tries again to lighten the atmosphere by describing Queen Mab, the Queen of the Fairies, who is believed to be responsible for people's dreams. Romeo has a premonition that he is about to do something that will have very serious consequences, but he decides nevertheless to go to the banquet.

Scene 5

The scene opens with some comic business from four Capulet servants preparing for the banquet. Capulet welcomes his guests and reminisces about dancing in his younger days. Romeo, wearing a mask to conceal his identity, notices Juliet for the first time, and is captivated by her beauty. Tybalt recognizes Romeo's voice, and is deeply offended that Romeo has come to the banquet. Capulet restrains him, mentioning Romeo's good reputation. Tybalt angrily leaves, swearing that he will take his revenge for Romeo's intrusion. Romeo encounters Juliet; they are immediately attracted to each other, and enjoy their first kiss.

The shared sonnet (and its religious language) indicate that the two are really meant for each other.

'Palm to palm is holy palmers' kiss'

Romeo discovers from the Nurse that Juliet is a
Capulet. Benvolio persuades Romeo to leave. Left
alone, Juliet finds out from the Nurse that Romeo
is from the hated Montague family. Both Romeo
and Juliet realize that they are in love with one of
their family's enemies.

Close reading: ll. 92–105

These lines are some of the most famous and important in the play.
Although in the form of a dialogue, they also have the form of a
sonnet. The first quatrain is spoken by Romeo and the second by
Juliet. The first, third and fourth lines of the third quatrain are
Romeo's; they then each have one line each of the couplet. Thus
Romeo has a little more than half of the sonnet and Juliet a little
less than half. The distribution and sequencing of lines reinforces
Romeo's role as the man making advances to the woman, with Juliet
at first matching Romeo's approach, quatrain for quatrain. But then
Romeo becomes more insistent, taking four of the last seven lines
as he overcomes Juliet's resistance, and finally kisses her. The
couplet (ll. 104–105), which would normally encapsulate the main
idea behind the sonnet, is split between the two characters, as Juliet
weakens slightly and then Romeo, seeing his opportunity, concludes
the argument, announcing that he will take the kiss.

They begin another sonnet (ll. 106–109), which is interrupted by the Nurse, bringing them sharply back to reality.

In striking contrast to his highly conventional expressions of adoration for Rosaline, Romeo's initial wooing of Juliet is witty at the same time as being subtly seductive; indeed it may be seductive precisely because it is witty. The seduction, which occurs in the space of 18 lines, relies on an extended metaphor which Romeo and Juliet share and develop. He depicts himself as a pilgrim who, having '*profaned*' the '*holy shrine*' by touching Juliet's hand, is ready to make amends '*with a tender kiss*'. Juliet immediately takes up the 'pilgrim' metaphor, telling him that his touch is not sinful, playing with the words '*palm*' and '*palmers*' (pilgrims were called 'palmers' because they brought back palm leaves as proof they been to the Holy Land) and telling him that truly devout pilgrims '*kiss*' by touching palms. Thus she does not submit to Romeo, but she does not discourage him either. Undeterred, Romeo keeps the metaphor going, protesting that palmers and even saints have lips as well as hands. Juliet protests that saints' and palmers' lips are meant for prayer. Romeo persists, claiming that a kiss will purge his sin. Juliet points out that saints (or their statues) remain unmoving, which gives Romeo the opportunity to tell her not to move while he kisses her. They return to the idea of sin, and the idea that by accepting his kiss, Juliet has absolved Romeo. He completes the verbal game by offering to reclaim his sin – i.e. to kiss her again.

The metaphor is supported and reinforced by a dense accumulation of religious vocabulary: *profane, holy shrine, sin, pilgrim, devotion, saints, holy palmers, prayer, pray, faith, grant, purged, trespass*. Several of these words are repeated, and the overall effect is of the language of religion being used as a kind of lovers' code. This is a striking reversal of the tradition that had existed in English poetry since the Middle Ages of religious poetry using the language of carnal love.

It seems extraordinary that this dialogue is the first exchange of words between Romeo and Juliet. It seems to have the function of a courtship ritual, or even a dance, taking the place of the dance that Romeo refuses to take part in. For this reason (and because this is a play), it would be worthwhile considering how the dialogue would be performed on stage. It is highly likely actors used gestures to convey this idea of a condensed courtship on stage. One possible series of gestures might be the following:

a) Romeo takes Juliet's hand in his – perhaps his right hand holding her left hand ('*If I profane with my unworthiest hand this holy shrine*').

b) Juliet moves her hand around so that the palm of her left hand touches the palm of Romeo's right hand in the form of hands in prayer ('*palm to palm is holy palmers' kiss*'). This would show their physical approach and still remain virtuous because of the prayer symbolism involved.

c) Romeo's wish for a kiss could be reinforced by his indicating their touching hands while saying '*let lips do what hands do*'.

d) He might then take back his hands and form them into a gesture of prayer ('*They pray; grant thou*').

e) Juliet adopts the role of an immobile statue allowing Romeo to actually kiss her.

In a play that is notable for the extreme compression of events, the intense and highly concentrated wordplay brings the lovers together much faster and with a deeper mutual attraction than any conventional dialogue could have done. Moreover, in the 1590s the sonnet was a very popular form of love poetry among the educated classes. Unlike most love sonnets, this sonnet does not speak about or address the beloved. Rather it is shared by the two lovers. This would indicate to the educated members of the audience that Romeo and Juliet are made for each other.

Prologue to Act Two

In another sonnet, the Chorus summarizes the story so far, telling us that Juliet has replaced Rosaline as the object of Romeo's affection, and reminding us of the danger he will be in if he attempts to continue the relationship.

Act Two

Scene 1
Romeo appears very briefly, consumed with passion for Juliet. Benvolio and Mercutio have followed him and have seen him climb a wall into Capulet's orchard. They call out to him, and in speeches that are full of sexual innuendo Mercutio speaks teasingly about Romeo's former love for Rosaline. Getting no reply from Romeo, he decides to go home to sleep.

Scene 2
Romeo hears Mercutio, but does not respond, as he thinks Mercutio can only joke about being in love because he has never experienced real love himself. Juliet appears at her bedroom window. Initially, Romeo is content just to look at her and is reluctant to address her until he hears her lamenting the fact that he is a Montague and

'O Romeo, Romeo! Wherefore art thou Romeo?'

wishing that they could both relinquish their names and be together. This gives Romeo the courage to speak: he declares his love and tells Juliet he is willing to reject his family for her sake. At first she is shocked to find him there. She warns him that the members of her family will kill him if they find him, but he insists that he would rather die than live without her love. This declaration of love is met with some caution by Juliet, who wants Romeo to swear that he loves her, but has some doubts about such outbursts. She wants to believe him, but at the same time she wants to hear something more deeply felt than the conventional language of the courtly lover. They are starting to explore more genuine ways of expressing their feelings for each other when Juliet is called in by the Nurse. The Nurse continues to call her as the lovers say goodnight. Juliet is almost convinced of Romeo's sincerity and tells him she will send a messenger the next day to find out if he wants to marry her. If he is serious, she says she will become his wife and follow him anywhere. Juliet withdraws, but almost immediately reappears, and they agree that her messenger will come to him at nine in the morning. Finally, they say goodnight.

Note that it is Juliet who tries to make Romeo express his love in sincere rather than conventional terms.

Sex before marriage was a taboo; getting married would prove Romeo's sincerity.

Scene 3

Friar Laurence, a Franciscan priest, has been gathering flowers and herbs. In a soliloquy full of oppositions, he reflects that people, like herbs that can poison or can heal, are capable of both good and evil. When Romeo appears, clearly not having been to bed, Friar Laurence suspects that he has spent the night with Rosaline. Romeo explains how he and Juliet have fallen head over heels in love and how they plan to marry

The friar states that good and evil are present in every-thing and are in a perpetual fight.

'Virtue itself turns vice, being misapplied'

immediately. After criticizing the rapid change in Romeo's affections, Friar Laurence agrees to solemnize the marriage, in the hope that their union will put an end to the destructive feud between the two families.

Scene 4

Benvolio tells Mercutio that Tybalt has challenged Romeo to a duel. Mercutio mocks Tybalt's fussy style of fencing and jokes that Romeo is already dead, killed by Cupid's arrow (i.e. by love). Thinking that Romeo is still besotted with Rosaline, Mercutio teasingly tells him that Cleopatra, Helen of Troy and other legendary beauties were plain and unattractive by comparison. Mercutio draws Romeo into a light-hearted exchange of jokes, full of sexual innuendo. When the Nurse appears, looking for Romeo, Mercutio continues his sexual banter, teasing her instead of Romeo. Before he departs, Mercutio sings a bawdy song directed at the Nurse, which she complains about. She warns Romeo not to mislead Juliet, but is quickly convinced of his sincerity. He tells her of his plan for Friar Laurence to marry them that afternoon and says he will send a servant with a rope ladder to enable him to climb up to Juliet's room. The Nurse assures Romeo that Juliet is devoted to him and detests his rival, Paris.

Scene 5

Juliet impatiently awaits the Nurse's return. She compares the swiftness of young love with the slow pace of the old. The Nurse arrives, complaining about her aching bones and breathlessness. She continues to complain and withhold her news, as Juliet becomes increasingly frustrated, wanting to know what message Romeo has sent. Finally, the Nurse tells her of Romeo's plan for the secret marriage.

Scene 6

Romeo waits with Friar Laurence in his cell for Juliet's arrival. His anticipation of their joyful union seems to be overshadowed by thoughts of sorrow and '*love-devouring death*'. Friar Laurence counsels Romeo to moderate his passion and avoid violent emotions. When Juliet appears, Romeo declares his love for her in the most extravagant language, while she maintains that true love cannot be described, only experienced. Friar Laurence leads them off to be married.

Note once again how Juliet is more down to earth than Romeo in expressing her love.

Act Three

Scene 1

Benvolio, anticipating trouble, tries in vain to persuade Mercutio to get off the street. Mercutio jokingly accuses Benvolio of being the kind of man who is always looking for a fight. Tybalt

In his description of Benvolio, Mercutio is describing himself.

enters, with several other Capulets, looking for Romeo. Tybalt, intent on fighting Romeo, refuses to be provoked by Mercutio. But when Romeo appears, he rejects Tybalt's challenge: married to Juliet, he is now related to Tybalt, though he cannot reveal this yet. Mercutio, outraged at Romeo's refusal to fight, challenges Tybalt himself. Romeo attempts to come between them, but his intervention gives Tybalt the opportunity to deliver a fatal thrust. Mortally wounded, Mercutio curses both the Montagues and the Capulets ('*A plague o' both your houses*'). Romeo, overcome with guilt, feels that love has undermined his manliness. But when he learns that Mercutio is dead, he is determined to take his revenge, and he fights and kills Tybalt.

'O, I am fortune's fool!'

The Prince appears, together with Capulet, Montague and their wives. Lady Capulet wants a life for a life and demands Romeo's death. Benvolio explains the sequence of events that led to the deaths of Mercutio and Tybalt, but Lady Capulet accuses him of partiality and again demands Romeo's execution. The Prince agrees with Montague that there was some justification in Romeo avenging Mercutio's death, but for killing Tybalt he exiles Romeo from Verona.

Scene 2

Juliet, unaware of everything that has happened, longs for night and the consummation of her marriage. The Nurse arrives with the rope ladder, incoherently lamenting Tybalt's death at the hands of Romeo. Juliet misinterprets the news, and, thinking it is Romeo who is dead, wishes that she could join him. When she learns the truth, at first she curses Romeo for appearing beautiful but acting wickedly. But then, when the Nurse agrees, her attitude changes quite abruptly, and she jumps to Romeo's defence. She realizes that if Romeo had not killed Tybalt, then Romeo himself would have been killed, and she alternates between sorrow at her cousin's death and desperation at her husband's banishment. When she threatens to kill herself, the Nurse promises to find Romeo and send him to say goodbye to her.

Scene 3

Friar Laurence brings Romeo news of the Prince's sentence of exile. For Romeo this is tantamount to a death sentence: life for him is only in Verona with Juliet, and 'world's exile is death'. Friar Laurence tells him he should be grateful for the Prince's mercy, but Romeo rejects Friar Laurence's 'philosophy' and refuses to be comforted. Romeo, full of self-pity, collapses on the floor and remains there despite Friar Laurence's pleas to him to stand up. Only when the Nurse arrives with news of Juliet does Romeo get up. But when he hears of Juliet's grief and tears, he threatens to stab himself. The Nurse takes the dagger away from him, and Friar Laurence first criticizes his unmanly behaviour and accuses him of killing his love; then he suggests that Romeo should count his blessings: Juliet is alive, Tybalt – instead of Romeo – is dead, and Romeo has been banished – instead of being executed; and finally, he outlines a plan for Romeo to accept his exile until the time is right to beg for a pardon and the right to return. Friar Laurence tells Romeo to go to Juliet as planned, but to make sure that he leaves for Mantua before the Watch come on duty. The Nurse gives Romeo a ring from Juliet and Friar Laurence promises to keep Romeo informed and to let him know when it might be safe to return.

Scene 4

Capulet tells Paris that because of Tybalt's death he has not yet spoken to Juliet about Paris's proposal of marriage. Capulet is sure that Juliet will obey him, and decides that she will marry Paris in three days' time. He wants it to be a quiet wedding with just a small group of friends, as he feels a big wedding celebration would be inappropriate so soon after Tybalt's death.

Scene 5

After Romeo and Juliet have spent their wedding night together, she tries to persuade him that he does not have to leave as it is not yet day. Seeing the dawn light, at first he is determined to go, but when Juliet insists, he says he will stay and face death for her sake. But on hearing this, Juliet says that it is indeed morning and time for him to leave. The Nurse comes to warn them that Juliet's

'I must be gone and live, or stay and die'

mother is approaching. Romeo leaves; Juliet wonders whether they will ever meet again and she has a premonition of Romeo dead in a tomb.

Lady Capulet assumes that Juliet is grieving for Tybalt's death. Juliet encourages this belief to the point where her mother promises to have Romeo poisoned in Mantua, where he has been exiled. The deception continues until Lady Capulet tells her daughter of the plan for her to marry Paris in two days' time. Juliet is horrified and with deliberate irony, tells her mother that she would rather marry Romeo, whom her mother knows she hates. Capulet enters and, like his wife, assumes that Juliet's tears are for Tybalt. When he hears of her refusal to marry Paris, he is furious and threatens to throw her out on the street. The Nurse attempts to defend Juliet, but only succeeds in provoking Capulet to greater anger. Juliet appeals to her mother, but Lady Capulet ignores her pleas.

Juliet seeks advice and support from the Nurse, who disappoints her by recommending marriage to Paris. At this point, Juliet realizes that she is on

Juliet uses language to deflect the truth.

Contrary to what he says in I, ii, it seems that her father, and not Juliet, will decide who she should marry.

her own. She sends the Nurse to tell her mother that she has gone to confession at Friar Laurence's. She hopes he will able to help her, but if all else fails, she feels she can at least have control of her life by deciding to die.

Act Four

Scene 1

In a dialogue that recapitulates what the audience already knows, Paris tells Friar Laurence of the plan to bring the wedding forward by a day. He also tells the Friar that Juliet's father hopes that the wedding will help her to overcome her grief at Tybalt's death. Juliet arrives and when Paris tries to discuss their wedding, she responds with answers that are full of double meanings that make sense to Friar Laurence – and the audience –

Once again Juliet uses language to hide her feelings.

'Take thou this vial'

but which Paris does not understand. When Paris departs, Juliet asks Friar Laurence for his help. She tells him she would rather kill herself than be married to Paris. Friar Laurence devises a plan, which will involve her pretending to be dead. She assures him that she is prepared to do anything if it will unite her with Romeo, and Friar Laurence tells her to make sure she goes to bed alone the following night. He gives her a small medicine container and explains to her – and the audience – that the liquid in the bottle will make her appear to be dead, but that after 42 hours she will regain consciousness. The plan is for her to be laid to rest in the family tomb, where Romeo will meet her when she wakes and take her with him to Mantua.

Scene 2
Capulet, busy with preparations for the wedding, is delighted when Juliet appears to be repentant and declares herself ready to obey her father and marry Paris. He decides to bring the wedding forward to Wednesday – the next day.

Scene 3
Juliet sends her mother and the Nurse away, pretending that she needs to be alone to pray. Fearing the potion provided by Friar Laurence might not work, she is prepared to kill herself with a dagger rather than submit to marriage with Paris.

Scene 4
On the morning of the wedding the Capulet household is busy with preparations. Lady Capulet alludes, in an apparently light-hearted way, to her husband having been a womaniser in the past.

Capulet orders the servingmen to hurry to get everything ready, and sends the Nurse to wake Juliet.

Scene 5

The Nurse attempts repeatedly to wake Juliet. Eventually, she concludes that Juliet is dead and rouses the whole household. Juliet's mother and father are overcome with grief. Paris arrives with Friar Laurence and joins the Capulets in mourning for Juliet. Friar Laurence, who alone knows that Juliet is not really dead, tells the family that they should stop lamenting Juliet's death as she is now in heaven. They all leave to prepare a funeral instead of a wedding.

Peter, the Nurse's servant, is left alone with the musicians, who had been employed to play at the wedding. He teases them with humorous insults, which they do not find at all amusing.

> Both Friar Laurence's speech and the musicians' chatter undermine the strong emotions that resulted from the Capulets' grief.

Act Five

Scene 1

Now in Mantua, Romeo reflects on a dream in which he was dead and a kiss from Juliet brought him back to life. His servant, Balthasar, arrives with the awful news of Juliet's death. Romeo sends Balthasar to hire horses and decides he will kill himself in the tomb where Juliet's body lies. He remembers an apothecary who illegally sells poisons and finds the apothecary's shop, which is shut for a holiday. The shopkeeper is reluctant to sell him poison, as he would face the death penalty if such a sale was discovered. But he is poor and Romeo offers him enough money to persuade him to take the risk.

Scene 2

Friar John, another Franciscan priest, arrives with the news that he has been unable to deliver Friar Laurence's letter to Romeo. The 'searchers', whose job was to prevent the spread of disease, suspected that he was in a house affected by the plague and would not allow him to leave Verona for Mantua. With his plan ruined, Friar Laurence decides to send another message to Romeo, then to go to the Capulet family tomb, rescue Juliet when she wakes and keep her safe until Romeo's return.

Scene 3

Paris comes to lay flowers at Juliet's tomb. He does not want to be seen and orders his page to keep watch. A whistle from the page warns him that someone (Romeo) is approaching the tomb. Romeo, like Paris, wants to be left alone, and he orders his servant, Balthasar, to withdraw. Balthasar, concerned about his master, decides to stay and watch. As Romeo begins to force the tomb open, he is challenged by Paris, who fears that he is about to desecrate Juliet's body. Romeo at first tries to avoid any conflict, but Paris provokes him and they fight. It is only after Paris dies that Romeo realizes who he has killed. Romeo fulfils Paris's dying request to have his corpse laid in the tomb next to Juliet's body.

Romeo is transfixed by Juliet's beauty. He asks Tybalt to forgive him and imagines Death wanting to be Juliet's lover. To keep Death away from her and be with her for ever, he drinks the poison and swiftly dies.

Close reading: ll. 88–120

The final dramatic irony in the play is Romeo's perception of Juliet's beauty lingering in death when we know that she is still alive. But the image of beauty preserved also suggests the transcendent quality of their love, which will outlive their deaths.

Romeo's last speech gathers together a number of images that have been used earlier in the play, adding to the feeling of finality and closure. The paradoxical idea of '*lightning before death*', a moment of joy '*at the point of death*', which Romeo emphatically rejects, brings to mind Juliet's fear (II, ii, 119–120) that their love would prove as brief-lived as a flash of lightning.

The image of Death as a bee, sucking the honey of Juliet's breath, reminds us of all the insect imagery in Mercutio's Queen Mab speech, and the '*infection*' of deceptive dreams – perhaps even of the plague with which Mercutio curses both families. Next Death becomes personified as a military leader, advancing on Juliet's beauty to plant his flag, an image which suggests that the frailty of Romeo and Juliet's love has been overcome by the violent antagonism between their families. Then Death actually supplants Romeo and becomes Juliet's lover (this reflects the personification of death as Juliet's husband by Capulet; IV, v, 38–39). This thought prompts the final paradox: the only way that Romeo can resist the power of Death as his rival for Juliet's love is to die himself, and thus be with her for ever. Here more creatures are mentioned – worms – but instead of fulfilling their conventional function of feeding on the corpse, they become Juliet's chambermaids, and an emblem of Romeo's triumph over death. In death Romeo will not only find '*everlasting rest*'; he will also '*shake the yoke of inauspicious stars*'. He sees himself here as overturning the very stars that have been responsible for his fate and that of Juliet. And with a final note of acceptance of the inevitable, rather than struggling any longer with Death, he enters into a '*dateless bargain*', an eternal contract with Death, sealed not with a handshake, but with the last kiss he gives to Juliet, a kiss which closes the circle that had begun with the kiss he had given her on their first meeting.

The last image of all, of Romeo's life as a ship out of control and dashed to pieces on the rocks, takes us back to Romeo's premonition of disaster to come in Act I, Scene 4, 106–113. It is worth reading these lines to compare them with Romeo's final acknowledgement of his fate, especially his plea that '*He that hath the steerage of my course direct my sail!*' The imagery in Act V ('*conduct*', '*guide*', '*pilot*', '*bark*') all emphasize the fact that Romeo sees his life as a sea journey ending in disaster. It is also worth noting that Romeo earlier told Juliet that '*I am no pilot, yet, wert thou as far as that vast shore washed with the farthest sea, I would adventure for such merchandise.*' (II, ii, 82–84). To a certain degree, by joining Juliet in death, he is keeping this promise.

Romeo's course has been steered onto the rocks, and the term of his life has expired. He and Juliet have been unable to escape their fate: all that remains is for him to drink the poison and die. But in his very last words – '*Thus with a kiss I die*' – there is one last verbal irony: in Elizabethan English 'die' was also a euphemism for a sexual climax, so dying with a kiss may also be seen as the lovers being united in passion as well as death.

Friar Laurence finally arrives, complaining to himself at how slowly he moves. Balthasar tells him that Romeo is already in the tomb and says he dreamed that Romeo had fought and killed someone. Friar Laurence enters the tomb and discovers the bodies of Romeo and Paris. Juliet wakes, wanting to know where Romeo is. Friar Laurence tells her that Romeo and Paris are both dead. He offers to take her to a convent and tries to persuade her to leave with him before they are caught by the Watch. Wanting to join Romeo in death, she refuses to leave. At first she wants to drink the same poison, but finds that Romeo has drunk it all. She even kisses him in the hope that there might still be some poison on his lips. She hears the Watch arriving and needing to act quickly, she grabs Romeo's dagger and stabs herself.

The Watch enter the tomb and discover the bodies of Romeo, Juliet and Paris. Not knowing what has happened, they arrest Balthasar and Friar Laurence. The Capulets arrive first, together with the Prince. The Captain of the Watch tells them as much as he can. The Capulets enter the tomb to see the bodies. Then Montague arrives and reports that his wife has died of grief over their son's exile. He, too, then sees the lifeless bodies. The Prince demands to know from those found in the churchyard exactly what has happened. Friar Laurence explains everything in detail and accepts his own responsibility – though he does not mention his intention to bring the two families together by helping the lovers. Balthasar and the page complete the story, and everything is corroborated by a letter written by

'A glooming peace this morning with it brings'

Romeo and given to Balthasar to deliver to his
father. The Prince rebukes Capulet and Montague
for the feud that has led to the deaths of their
children, and of others.

Capulet and Montague are reconciled, and
each promises to erect a golden statue of the
other's child. Finally, the Prince says there will be
pardon for some and punishment for others – but
he does not specify what kind of punishment or
for whom.

Characters ◄◄◄

Although all the characters in *Romeo and Juliet* have their individual personalities, they should also be seen in relation to their **families**. The play is built around the two opposing families, the Montagues and the Capulets, with the Prince and (to a lesser extent) Friar Laurence standing outside this conflict. Thus, to understand each of the characters, it is also important to know where they belong with regard to each other. The diagram on p. 48 should help you to do this, and it also shows how Shakespeare offers the audience a balanced group of characters.

While it might appear that the play is equally about the two families ('*Two households, both alike in dignity*', Prologue, 1), *Romeo and Juliet* is in fact more about the Capulets. After the death of Mercutio in Act III, Scene 1, the play is centred on the Capulet family. Neither Benvolio, Romeo's friend and a Montague, nor Romeo's parents return until the final scene, after the deaths of the lovers. It is not the case, though, that nothing happens in the Montague household. When Lord Montague does appear at the end of the play, he announces that his wife had died shortly beforehand (which may be because the boy actor playing Lady Montague was needed in another role in the final scene). We otherwise know very little about Lady Montague. She appears to exist solely to balance the two families. The emphasis on the Capulets serves to make Juliet a more prominent character than Romeo, as we see her in two settings – her own home and at Friar Laurence's cell. While Juliet, as a woman, has little freedom of movement outside the home, Romeo is always depicted outside his own home. Having fallen in love with Juliet, he becomes completely removed from his family and enters a no-man's land between the two warring factions, a place that is inevitably dangerous and where he cannot stay. Indeed he is banished, not merely from this middle ground, but from Verona itself.

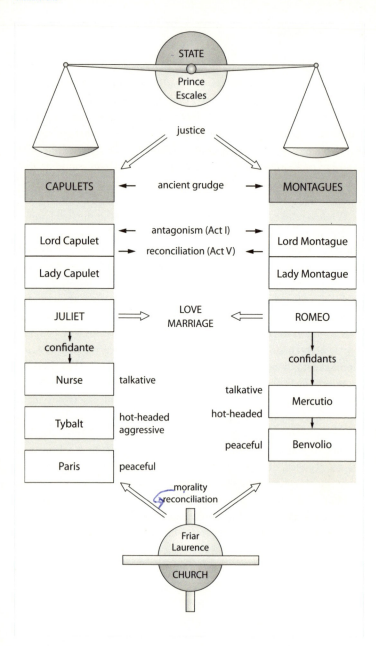

Romeo
Romeo's development

Romeo would appear, from the title of the play, to be the hero, yet we do not meet him until the end of the first scene, and our first impressions of him are not entirely favourable. In order to understand **Romeo's development** it is worth examining five major scenes:

1. Act I, Scene i, 153–230:

Romeo's parents are worried about his behaviour and when he arrives on stage, he seems to be **isolated and melancholy**. Shakespeare's audience would have considered that he had too much black bile (cf. 'Four Humours', p. 6), which his father also fears (I, i, 134), and that he was unbalanced because of this. Yet the concern felt by his family and friends would indicate that this melancholy is uncharacteristic, and Romeo confirms this. Because of his unreciprocated love for Rosaline, he has changed: '*I have lost myself; I am not here.*' (I, i, 190).

We encounter him here as the typical **courtly lover** who is suffering from **unrequited love from an unattainable woman**, Rosaline. One might say that he is in love with the concept of being in love rather than in love with Rosaline. His description of love in I, i, 181–187 uses stereotypical clichés about love, while his description of Rosaline in 201–217 emphasizes her rejection of his love, which makes his own desire grow stronger. While Rosaline might be an ideal object for the courtly lover, this is not a true love between partners. Romeo can only mope around feeling sorry for himself; appropriately, Romeo wanders around in the woods or locks himself up in his room. His love results in him being alone; true love involves partnership, interaction and companionship.

2. Act I, Scene v, 40–52, 92–109:

The meeting with Juliet changes Romeo. While he may come across as impetuous by falling so suddenly in love, from an audience's point of view this change is acceptable. Romeo directs his attention from the unseen Rosaline to the **visible Juliet**. While discussing Rosaline in Act I, Scene 2, Romeo makes use of language associated with 'sight', yet Rosaline is not seen (indeed Romeo refers to love as '*muffled*' and '*without eyes*', I, i, 164, 165). Here, Juliet is on stage, so the audience sees a real person who has aroused love in Romeo. Romeo realizes the artificiality of his love for Rosaline when he has a real lover in front of him ('*Did my heart love till now? Forswear it, sight! For I ne'er saw true beauty till this night.*', 51–52). The sonnet shared by Romeo and Juliet in 92–105 (and the second one started in 106–109) indicates that the love between the two is genuine. In the following scene (Act II, Scene 1) Romeo is forced by Juliet to abandon his exaggerated language of love and instead to take action.

3. Act III, Scene 1

This is the dramatic scene in which Mercutio is killed by Tybalt and in which Romeo takes revenge on Tybalt. Up to this point Romeo has been locked away in his private world of love. Romeo is not involved in the brawl in Act I, Scene 1 and indeed his comments on it (I, i, 166–168) indicate his inability to take it seriously. His love even takes him to the house of his enemy just to see his beloved. He is aware of the feud, but does not let it hinder him from pursuing his amorous desires. In this scene, however, his private world of love (now for Juliet) clashes with the public world of the feud. He places his love for Juliet above the need to fight his newly-acquired relative, Tybalt. His attempts to defuse the situation result in his clumsy interference and Mercutio's death. At this point he changes: his anger overcomes his feelings for Juliet and he kills Tybalt, thereby throwing himself into confusion. His perfect **world of love** has been broken by the outside **world of hatred**, and he gives the impression that he is no longer in command of his world ('*O, I am fortune's fool*', III, i, 135).

4. Act III, Scene 3

Banished from Verona and Juliet, Romeo returns to his characteristic immature disposition. He acts unreasonably and hysterically, wishing death on himself, rather than viewing his situation rationally. Perhaps more important is the fact that he worries that he has lost Juliet's love by killing her cousin. Romeo is **characterized throughout the play as a lover**. Should this love be over, his reason for being may be considered over. It is the reassurance of Juliet's love and the decisive plan of action proposed by the Friar that bring Romeo back to life, and make him able to act again. Indeed in the next scene in which he appears (Act III, Scene 5), Romeo is the mature husband and lover. Together with Juliet it seems he gains in stature; without her he seems lost and immature. Yet even here, it is Juliet who must force him to leave the bedchamber, so that he will not be caught and put to death.

5. Act V, Scene 3

On learning of Juliet's death Romeo displays a stoic calm which one might not expect from him. His words and actions correspond: he is prepared to join his lover in death, and he is respectful to those dead around him, Tybalt and Paris, both of whom he has killed, by requesting their forgiveness. His final speech reflects that he was always a **melancholic lover**, but here his melancholy is appropriate, as his real love is dead and he will soon be dead too.

Romeo as tragic hero

In his death scene Romeo reveals that he is a truly tragic hero. Historically, to be considered a tragic hero, the protagonist must come from a **noble family**, have some **feeling for his fate and destiny**, and possess an **inherent weakness** (often called a **tragic flaw**) that leads to his downfall and ultimate destruction. A tragic hero must be aware of his tragic destiny, and Shakespeare reveals, quite early on, Romeo's sense of foreboding as he goes to the fateful party where he will meet Juliet and seal his fate: '*my mind misgives some consequence yet hanging in the stars shall bitterly begin his fearful date with this night's revels and expire the term of a despised life closed in thy breast by some vile forfeit of untimely death*' (I, iv, 106–111).

As to what his tragic flaw might be, there is no simple answer. It may be his **passivity**. Romeo has been changed by love, and it is love itself, personified as a tyrant, which dominates his thoughts. Throughout the play he reacts rather than acts. He is always more inclined to think about poetry and witty exchanges with his friends than practical considerations about, for example, the marriage. It is

Juliet who sends her Nurse to find out what steps he has taken and who instigates the action. Romeo reacts to the actions of others. He kills Tybalt, because he is furious at the death of his closest friend, Mercutio, and because of the guilt he feels in not responding to Tybalt's challenge. His response to his banishment is despair, and both Friar Laurence and the Nurse accuse him of not behaving like a man at this point in the play. Finally, when he hears of Juliet's death, he immediately seeks his own.

Other critics feel that if Romeo does have a flaw, it is not so much passivity, but **youthful impetuosity**. Passionate and impetuous, he never stops to think of the implications of his actions, a sign perhaps that Shakespeare saw him as a very young man. He instantly falls out of love with Rosaline and in love with Juliet. He rushes into his marriage with Juliet (but this ignores the fact that it is Juliet who proposes marriage, not Romeo). Yet it is this impetuosity and passion that allows Romeo to give himself totally to Juliet. Because of this, we believe completely in his love for her and because of this, his death seems truly tragic. Only with Juliet does he seem to gain maturity, yet even here it is not always the case. His language always tends towards dangerous hyperbole, e.g. on his marriage he states '*then love-devouring death do what he dare*' (II, vi, 7).

Any actor playing Romeo must address the problems inherent in his character. It is because of these problems that so many directors have changed the text to make Romeo appear stronger and more in charge of his destiny. The famous actor David Garrick rewrote the play in the 18th century, removing Rosaline (as well as much of Mercutio's part) so that he could play Romeo as a 'true' hero. He did not want Romeo to appear weak. Contemporary actors, on the other hand, often portray him as a moody teenager.

However, the essence of a tragic hero is one who can change, and Romeo does indeed change when he meets Juliet. After so much anguish, at first he hardly dares to believe that he can be so happy: '*I am afeard. [...] All this is but a dream, too flattering-sweet to be substantial.*' (II, ii, 139–141). His joy causes him to rush instantly into marriage (see 'Time', p.73), but in finding Juliet he also finds himself. '*Now art thou sociable; now art thou Romeo*' says Mercutio (II, iv, 83), enjoying his friend's wit once again.

▶ **Revision**
(what you learn about Romeo)

- Romeo is the embodiment, at the beginning, of the courtly lover, and later of the male lover in general.
- On meeting Juliet, Romeo is forced to reconsider his views of love.
- Romeo is introduced as melancholic person with a tendency to exaggeration. He never quite loses these traits during the course of the play.
- Romeo is a tragic hero, who is aware of his struggle with destiny and who possesses character faults like passivity and impetuosity.

A few important quotes	
Quote	**Analysis**
Black and portentous must this humour prove, Unless good counsel may the cause remove. (I, i, 134–135) *Griefs of mine own lie heavy in my breast* (I, i, 179) *Under love's heavy burden do I sink* (I, iv, 22)	Romeo is suffering from melancholy, as he is in love but his lover does not return his love.
Did my heart love till now? Forswear it, sight! For I ne'er saw true beauty till this night. (I, v, 51–52)	Romeo falls instantly in love with Juliet.
a virtuous and well-governed youth (I, v, 67)	Romeo is recognized even by his enemies as being a good person.
Call me but love, and I'll be new baptised; Henceforth I never will be Romeo. (II, ii, 50–51)	Romeo puts love above all other considerations, even his family.

Lady, by yonder blessed moon I swear *That tips with silver all these fruit-tree tops* (II, ii, 107–108)	He never quite manages to escape from his use of exaggerated love language.
But He that hath the steerage of my course *Direct my sail!* (I, iv, 112–113) *I am fortune's fool* (III, i, 135)	Romeo views his fate as being not in his own hands.
Well, Juliet, I shall lie with thee tonight. (V, i, 34) 　　　　　　*here* *Will I set up my everlasting rest,* *And shake the yoke of inauspicious stars* *From this world-wearied flesh.* (V, iii, 109–112)	On learning of Juliet's death, Romeo is determined to join her in death.

Vocabulary: talking about Romeo

- courtly lover, unrequited love, ideal(ized) lover
- melancholic, inexperienced, moody, brooding
- passive, reacts to events
- impetuous, passionate, reckless
- amiable, affable, likeable, popular, enjoys verbal jousting
- virtuous, charming, attentive
- prone to outbursts, uses exaggerated poetic language, hysterical

Juliet

It is not surprising that of all Shakespeare's heroines, the part perhaps most prized by actresses is that of Juliet. It is not simply that she is **beautiful and brave**, but also she is unusually strong and quick-thinking. In a patriarchal society, she emerges as the one character who is determined not to submit to society's rules and who has the **determination and strength** to do what she wants. She marries secretly and dies rather than submit to an arranged marriage. Yet Juliet remains problematic for directors, as her character is said to be almost fourteen, yet the part demands an emotional depth and understanding of poetry that few actresses have at that age. Originally, of course, her part was played by a boy actor, and once again this underscores the fact that realism was not the aim in Shakespeare's day. These plays presented a juxtaposition of ideas developed through character.

While it was unusual for a heroine in this period to be so dynamic, it was not unknown in the poetry of the time. Mercutio (II, iv, 39–43) lists some of the heroines celebrated by Petrarch, who would have been familiar to many in the audience. These include Cleopatra, a powerful and strong queen; Helen, who left her husband to be with her lover; and Thisbe, who loved her family's enemy Pyramus, and died because of this – a precursor of the Romeo and Juliet story. Moreover, at the time, England was ruled by Elizabeth I, a practical and forceful woman in a man's world. The difference between these women and Juliet lies in the domestic, non-mythological and non-political world in which the character Juliet is to be found. Her house, her family and herself are easily identifiable to the audience as being part of the English social landscape (even if the play is set in Italy).

It is often said that the true nature of a character is seen when they are put under pressure, and this is certainly true in Juliet's case. She changes from a quiet, dutiful child, who it seems has never been outside her own home, into a practical, passionate lover and a determined tragic heroine who, when let down by all around her, is able to take a terrible and irreversible decision.

We first hear of Juliet in a conversation between her father and Paris in Act I, Scene 2. Her youth is emphasized – her father thinks she is too young to be married. When we meet Juliet, it is within the enclosed world of the Capulet household. She is portrayed as an indulged child. To her father, following the death of his other children, she is *'the hopeful lady of my earth'* (I, ii, 15). Her mother wants her to have a good match and her Nurse, who is closest to her, adores the girl who was *'the prettiest babe'* (I, iii, 62), simply wanting her to be happy. Juliet has been kept safe inside the home and at the beginning of the play says she has never thought of marriage. She is a child. Yet the concept of childhood in Elizabethan England was very different from how we understand the term today: it was mostly a time to learn how to behave, and the most important rule was to obey and show reverence to one's parents. Thus Juliet answers correctly that marriage is *'an honour that I dream not of'* (I, iii, 68).

Yet within a few hours she is breaking all the rules that she has been taught. At her father's party she meets Romeo and falls in love, initiating the change from an innocent child into a married and determined woman. But even in later scenes with her parents, she never stops her obedience, playing with words to hide the truth from her mother and Paris, regretting the hurt she causes in her father. She only refuses her father's demands when he insists on her marrying Paris, an act she cannot carry out, as she is already married.

It is important to remember that this play is about love, and convention insists that the girl is described in terms of **beauty**. Romeo's first words describing her indicate that she has taken his breath away, as he begins his eulogy with an exclamation: *'O, she doth teach the torches to burn bright! It seems she hangs upon the cheek of night like a rich jewel in an Ethiop's ear. Beauty too rich for use, for earth too dear.'* (I, v, 43–46). Remembering that the part was played by a boy, this reveals how important the role of language was in conveying ideas (even of beauty); on stage Juliet need not be too beautiful, it is Shakespeare's language that makes her so. In this passage Juliet is described as sticking out (white/light against dark/night). Once her beauty is established, it is only referred to again at the end: '*Death […] hath had no power yet upon thy beauty.*' (V, iii, 92–93).

On meeting Romeo, it is her knowledge of how to play the game of love that surprises. The innocent girl from the previous scene has vanished to be replaced by a young girl suddenly aware of her emotional needs. She encourages Romeo ('*For saints have hands that pilgrims' hands do touch*', I, v, 98, i.e. he may touch her) but insists she will only react to his actions ('*Saints do not move, though grant for prayers' sake*', I, v, 104). Juliet is always aware of her female role as the traditional object of affection who has more to lose than the man.

In Act II, Scene 2, she battles with the social conventions and with her desires, which she has inadvertently revealed to Romeo: in ll. 85–106 she gives a remarkable speech in which acknowledges she has broken convention by not playing 'hard to get', which may lower her in Romeo's eyes. It is too late for her to follow social custom, as she might have done in different circumstances: '*Fain would I dwell on form, fain, fain deny what I have spoke: but farewell compliment!*' (88–89) but then says '*I'll prove more true than those that have more coying to be strange*' (100–101). Juliet basically tells Romeo she loves him, although she blushes at being so outspoken, and is worried by the speed of their love: '*It is too rash, too unadvised, too sudden*' (118). She clearly sees the danger of this sudden romance, but is too in love with Romeo to allow these fears to dominate. Yet she knows their love is vital: '*This bud of love […] may prove a beauteous flower when next we meet.*' (121–122). At this point she is prepared to leave their love where it is, with the exchange of lovers' vows. When Romeo insists on more, she then asks for a clear response from Romeo and for him to act, not merely talk: '*If that thy bent of love be honourable, thy purpose marriage, send me word tomorrow.*' (143–144). If their love is to have a future, it must be sealed within marriage. Juliet has already reached the logical conclusion that Romeo has not thought of. Within twenty-four hours she is married to him. Throughout this scene her **practicality** is contrasted with Romeo's dreaminess. While Romeo talks to her with the extended metaphors of courtly love, she asks him directly how he got into her parents' orchard and warns him of the dangers of being there. When she asks Romeo directly if he loves her as she does him, he continues to use poetic imagery. She twice interrupts him as he is about to be effusive with his language, first telling him not to swear by the moon, and then not to swear at all.

We are reminded that she is still young by her **impatience** both to find out what Romeo feels and (later in Act II, Scene 5) when she becomes irritated that the Nurse takes too long to return from meeting Romeo and then to tell her what he said. However, in Act III, Scene 2, her impatience after her marriage but before spending her first night with Romeo is less child-like and demonstrates a mature passion. She even compares her impatience to that of a child before a holiday (29–31), suggesting that she herself is no longer a child.

It is in this scene that we see how quickly she has grown up, and we observe the stages of that development. First, after learning of Tybalt's death, she reveals her confused feelings, as her husband has killed her cousin and she does not know how to react. Finally, however, she realizes her loyalties lie with her husband and rebukes the Nurse for slandering Romeo. Later, after the Nurse suggests she should marry Paris, Juliet excludes the Nurse from her confidence. The Nurse was the one person she trusted but she has let her down when Juliet most needed help. From now on Juliet is on her own. This is the turning point for Juliet as all the ties to her home have been cut and she must make her own decisions. In Act IV, Scene 3, she considers the possibility that the Friar may actually be trying to kill her with the potion and the fact that she may wake up locked in a tomb surrounded by skeletons and ghosts (in Elizabethan times more frightening than today). This is her final test, but she proves unwavering and loyal to her husband. It is this strength that takes her all the way to her final suicide.

▶ **Revision**
(what you learn about Juliet)
- Juliet develops from an innocent child into a determined woman.
- Juliet is a practical person whose passion and temperament push the action forward.
- Nevertheless, she can be impatient and impetuous, as can be seen in the two scenes where she waits for news concerning Romeo.
- Her actions are limited by the confines of the house. As a woman she does not enjoy the freedom which a man would enjoy.

A few important quotes

Quote	Analysis
She is the hopeful lady of my earth (I, ii, 15)	Juliet is the only child and hope of the Capulet family.
It is an honour that I dream not of (I, iii, 68)	Her response to the marriage plans show her obedience but reveal her vagueness.
Saints do not move, though grant for prayers' sake (I, v, 104)	Juliet encourages Romeo's advances.
If thou dost love, pronounce it faithfully (II, ii, 94)	Juliet demands that Romeo speaks plainly and clearly.
I'll prove more true Than those that have more coying to be strange (II, ii, 100–101)	Juliet knows her feelings and is willing to state them clearly.
If that thy bent of love be honourable, Thy purpose marriage, send me word tomorrow (II, ii, 143–144)	She makes Romeo propose marriage.
Shall I speak ill of him that is my husband? (III, ii, 97) *Go, counsellor. Thou and my bosom henceforth shall be twain.* (III, v, 240–241)	She is loyal to her husband and cuts herself off from others as part of her commitment to him.

vocabulary: talking about Juliet

- impetuous, impatient, changes moods easily
- sanguine, practical, pragmatic, strong-minded, takes the initiative
- uses words to reveal/conceal things
- dutiful daughter, obedient to her parents' will
- steadfast in her devotion to her husband, loyal

Capulet

Lord Capulet is a man full of contradictions, and of all the nobility, apart from the two protagonists, his is the character which is most fully developed. He is a traditional Elizabethan nobleman, the head of a household, keen to show off his wealth and improve the status of his family through an advantageous marriage. His servant calls him '*the great rich Capulet*' (I, ii, 80–81). Juliet is his only remaining daughter, and it is his responsibility to find a suitable match for her. Some modern  readers have complained that he behaves as if Juliet is his property, but we should remember that to a certain extent she is: in Elizabethan England children were the property of their parents, just as wives were the property of their husbands. Yet it is clear at the opening of the play that Capulet wants the best for his daughter. He will only accept Paris as a suitor if Juliet agrees. He suggests to Paris that he should look at the other girls at the feast as well as Juliet. As a doting father, he suspects that Paris will choose his daughter, but he wants Paris to choose her because he likes her, not just because it is a suitable match. He urges him to '*get her heart*' (I, ii, 16).

His next appearance is as a generous host, who enjoys watching the women dancing, though he is too old to dance himself. His reminiscences in Act I, Scene 5, 29–39 make him both sympathetic and immediately identifiable as a character. Moreover, he is generous when it is revealed that Romeo has come to his house as a masked reveller, and comments that Romeo is well regarded in Verona and he would therefore never be discourteous to him. Capulet is very conscious of his social standing, as can be seen in the way in which he interferes in the kitchens to ensure that there is enough food for his guests. He is very conscious of social manners and customs, referring to Romeo as a gentleman and to the rude and aggressive Tybalt in l.76 as a '*goodman boy*' (a young yeoman who is below the status of a gentleman). Tybalt's desire to fight Romeo and disrupt his feast makes him furious. It is at this point that we see how violent and angry he can become when his authority is challenged. This will prove to be disastrous for Juliet when he decides that she must marry Paris immediately and she refuses.

One insight into Capulet's relationship with his wife is given in Act Four. Playing with a pun on 'watching', she says that he was a womaniser in his day, but she will watch him to prevent him flirting in the future: '*you have been a mouse-hunt in your time*' (IV, iv, 11). His reply that she is jealous may either be teasing or irritated. This depends entirely on how the line is spoken and on how a director wishes to portray the marriage. In any event, it reveals the normal banter between a husband and wife who have been married for many years.

Capulet's extreme anger when Juliet disobeys him is matched by his grief when she dies. Everything that he wanted has been destroyed and he is devastated by her death. He acts in what he believes are Juliet's best interests, but does not know the whole story (indeed discovering she is already married would probably have made him even more angry). Without his impulsive move to bring forward Juliet's marriage to Paris, the two lovers would not have died. But Shakespeare makes Capulet much more than a figure whose purpose is simply to move the plot along. He is a complex character whose behaviour demonstrates the constraints of the world in which Romeo and Juliet lived.

Lady Capulet

The role of a noblewoman in Elizabethan England was to remain at home and ensure that her children were correctly brought up. Marriage for love was rare, although it was not considered improper for love to develop within a marriage. There are few clues as to how Lady Capulet feels about her older husband, although the sarcasm in her first speech, when she suggests he would do better with a crutch than a sword (I, i, 69), might make us think that they are not the happiest of couples. Her duty is to obey her husband, whether or not she agrees with his decisions. While Lady Capulet cannot understand Juliet's refusal to marry Paris, she does not sympathize with Lord Capulet's treatment of her (III, v, 157, 175). She is annoyed, too, when her husband changes the wedding from Thursday to early Wednesday morning. He brushes away her protests, showing that she has no power in this relationship. In her first scene with Juliet, she is understandably impatient with the Nurse's chattering and frequently sounds both annoyed and exhausted.

Apart from her relationship with her husband, her main purpose is to ensure that her daughter marries well. Obviously, her husband informs her of Paris's interest. As a woman conscious of social status, she knows that Paris would be a good match. She then urges Juliet to consider Paris as a potential husband, using the metaphor of a book (I, iii, 83–94). When Juliet refuses to marry Paris (Act III, Scene 5), Lady Capulet has little sympathy with her, but nevertheless cannot understand her husband's choleric reaction.

It is perhaps not surprising that her character is only sketched in, as in the original texts she is variously called 'Lady of the House', 'Old Lady', 'Lady' Wife' or 'Mother'. It is contemporary editors who have tidied this up and named her 'Lady Capulet' throughout. The fact that one of her names is 'Old Lady' reminds us that at the end of the play she speaks of her '*old age*' (V, iii, 207). It is quite possible that Shakespeare forgot that in an earlier scene she says that she was Juliet's age when Juliet was born, thus making her only about twenty-eight. These plays were written quickly for performance; Shakespeare would have been amazed to find they were being studied closely some four hundred years later.

The Nurse

The Nurse (we are never sure about her name) belongs – like Peter and the other servingmen in this play – to a tradition of comic servants which goes back to classical Greece literature. They are talkative and disrespectful, and their language is full of sexual innuendo. The Nurse is a sympathetic character and one of the most fully realized in the play. Her direct colloquial prose is in strong contrast to the formal or poetic speech of those around her. We get the impression that she has been a member of the Capulet household for a long time – prior to nursing Juliet, she may have brought up Lord or Lady Capulet – and this gives her the freedom to address both of Juliet's parents quite informally. When Lord Capulet is preparing for the wedding, her scolding '*Go, you cot-quean, go, get you to bed. Faith, you'll be sick tomorrow for this night's watching.*' (IV, iv, 6–8) makes her sound like his nurse or his wife.

The Nurse is Juliet's only confidante, and it would have been her duty to bring her up and educate her in correct behaviour up to the moment when Juliet was old enough to join adult society. It is she who breast-fed Juliet and, almost like a mother, she recalls Juliet's childhood with pleasure (Act I, Scene 3). Her long-winded story about Juliet falling down and the impatience shown by Lady Capulet and Juliet as she tells the story indicates that they may have heard it often before.

The Nurse helps Juliet to marry Romeo secretly and by deceiving the Capulets, the Nurse breaks the trust between her and the family. She then breaks Juliet's trust in her after Romeo has been banished by suggesting that Juliet marry Paris. Juliet is left totally isolated, and this betrayal leads her to stop confiding in the Nurse. After Juliet takes the potion, the Nurse, like Juliet's parents, believes that she is dead. And this is the last time we see the Nurse.

Friar Laurence

Our first impressions of the Friar are of a healer and a philosopher. He is gathering herbs to use as medicine and at the same time he reflects on the properties of the plants, which can be both beneficial and harmful, to make the point that there is also good and bad in men. It is his desire to heal the rift between the two families that encourages him to marry Romeo and Juliet in secret and then try to protect Juliet from a marriage to Paris.

He is Romeo's confidant (mirroring the relationship of the Nurse and Juliet) and has possibly tutored him. The Friar calls Romeo his '*good son*' and his '*pupil*' (II, iii, 47, 82). Friar Laurence is not just a Franciscan but also an ordained priest who can absolve sins and perform marriages. Both Romeo and Juliet seem to have a deep trust in him, following all his plans, no matter how strange and dangerous they may seem.

His slowness shows his age, in contrast to the swiftness of the young couple, and his advice to act slowly and calmly is ignored both by Romeo and Juliet, and by Lord Capulet.

His actions, however, may be seen to be misguided, so that he comes across as an ambiguous figure. While he is twice referred to as '*a holy man*' (IV, iii, 29 and V, iii, 270), he plots in a way that brings great grief to the Capulets, as they believe their daughter is dead (Act IV, Scene 5). When Juliet awakens in the tomb, his first reaction is to put her in a convent in order to hide the shame, and his second reaction is to flee in order not to get caught. Of course, these actions are all necessary to enable the tragedy to unfold, and it would be a little unfair to judge him as a real person rather than as a figure in a tragedy. Indeed, the Friar does accept responsibility for the two deaths. When the Prince announces at the end that some will be punished (V, iii, 308), we wonder whether the Friar will be one of these.

Mercutio

Mercury was the messenger of the gods, and was responsible for dreams and visions. The adjective 'mercurial' means lively, witty and fast-talking, and indeed Mercutio is the most scintillating character in the play. In many ways Mercutio takes away much of the attention from Romeo, and some critics have suggested that Shakespeare kills Mercutio halfway through the play because he is such an attractive character that there is a danger of him overshadowing the melancholy Romeo. But his death has a more important dramatic function: it takes away Romeo's support, leaving him isolated, and also shifts the emphasis of the play to the world of the Capulets.

Audiences in Shakespeare's day would certainly have appreciated the wordplay at which Mercutio excels. He puns relentlessly, even at the moment of his death: '*ask for me tomorrow, and you shall find me a grave man*' (III, i, 96–97). Mercutio stands outside the feud between the Capulets and Montagues, as he is a relative of the Prince, but he fights on Romeo's behalf as a friend and because he dislikes Tybalt's affectations. His role is also to provide an opposite view of love from that of Romeo. He counters Romeo's protestations of courtly love with a direct and earthy humour, full of sexual innuendo. But once Romeo has replaced his empty, unrequited love for Rosaline with a real, consummated passion for Juliet, Mercutio's comments are no longer necessary.

Benvolio

'*I do but keep the peace*' (I, i, 61), says Benvolio. His name means 'well-wishing', and his role in the play is that of the peacemaker. He is the first noble character we meet, and we first see him trying to stop the servants from fighting. He is then asked by Romeo's parents to find out why Romeo is so unhappy. It is he who suggests going to Capulets' feast so that Romeo might find another love to replace his unrequited passion for Rosaline. This is intended to be a way of lifting Romeo out of his melancholy and is one of the many ironies in the play, as it leads to the lovers' encounter and ultimately their deaths. When Romeo and Mercutio go to the Capulets' feast, it is Benvolio who tries to avoid problems. He tells his companions that they should go in and perform the customary dance immediately (I, iv, 33–34), and it is he who tries to prevent Mercutio from walking around the city when the danger of a brawl exists (III, i, 1–4) and to stop Tybalt from fighting (III, i, 49–52). His speech to the Prince after the deaths of Tybalt and Mercutio saves Romeo's life. He blames Tybalt for starting the fight and underlines the fact that Mercutio, killed by Tybalt, was a relative of the Prince, '*thy kinsman, brave Mercutio*' (III, i, 144). Along with other members of the Montague clan, he is not seen after this, which underlines Romeo's isolation.

Tybalt

When we first meet Tybalt (I, i, 59–65), he threatens to kill Benvolio and boasts how he hates both peace and the Montagues. His hatred acts as a background and contrast to the love in the play. He simmers with fury when Lord Capulet prevents him from fighting Romeo at the feast and is determined to challenge Romeo to a duel. Romeo's refusal to fight him leads to the death of Mercutio, and the tragic outcome of the play. Tybalt is a stock character, the personification of choler and anger. Mercutio portrays Tybalt as posturing and affected, someone who duels according to the latest rules of fashion, but who does not really know how to fight (Act II, Scene 4). He mocks him as a '*rat-catcher*' and a '*Prince of cats*', since the name 'Tibault' comes from a Dutch fable about a princely cat. Tybalt was a common English name for a cat in Shakespeare's day (just as its derivative, 'Tibbles', is for cats today). Ironically, when Mercutio and Tybalt do fight, Tybalt kills Mercutio not through his swordsmanship but through the clumsy interference of Romeo. Shortly after, Romeo kills him. Despite his words and aggression, Tybalt's courage and skill do not amount to much.

Paris

'*Verona's summer hath not such a flower*', says Lady Capulet (I, iii, 79). It would have been easy for Shakespeare to gain the sympathy of the audience by portraying Juliet's suitor as an old or unattractive man, but the playwright does not do this. Paris is young, attractive, charming and eligible, and his love for Juliet appears to be genuine, as can be seen by his visit to her tomb after her 'death'. This makes Juliet's decision not to marry him harder and increases the audience's sympathy for her. Paris is a relation of Prince Escales, and his marriage to Juliet offers the Capulet family the chance to rise in society. When he talks to Lord Capulet about the two families, he says: '*Of honourable reckoning are you both*' (I, ii, 4), thus giving the impression that his status is higher than either. Yet he shares the fate of Romeo and Juliet. As Romeo says of him, he is '*One writ with me in sour misfortune's book*' (V, iii, 82).

The Prince

The name of Prince Escales ('scales') gives us a clue to the role of his character. He is the personification of justice and the law. The image of justice with a sword in one hand and the scales in the other is an ancient one, and one embodied by the Prince. While he has few lines and only appears three times in the play – at the beginning, in the middle and at the end – his influence is felt throughout. The power which he exerts within Verona is absolute, both over the nobles and the church. When he banishes Romeo, Romeo has to leave instantly to avoid being executed. This power echoes the role of the State in England in Shakespeare's day following the weakening of the power of the Church. The Prince's role is to bring order and prevent the civil unrest which threatens to erupt throughout the play: '*For now, these hot days, is the mad blood stirring*' (III, i, 4). Shakespeare's wish for national order to be sustained and his fear of anarchy is evident in many of his plays.

The Servants

The comedy and sexual humour of the servants act as a bridge between scenes of high drama. It is known that the famous clown Will Kemp played Peter, and it seems probable that he also played many of the other comic servants who are not named, such as one of the servingmen in IV, ii, 1–8, in I, v and the servant who cannot read the names of the guests in I, ii, 38–83.

▶▶▶ Themes

All the themes in *Romeo and Juliet* come in pairs:

- love and hate
- fate and free will
- youth and age
- masculinity and femininity.

For every idea in the play you can discover its opposite; so for example, while much of the play is about two young people, there are also many references to old age. In addition to the pairs of opposites discussed below, you can also find examples of other pairs such as 'light/dark' and 'public/private'. Even events become their opposites: a wedding feast becomes a funeral. '*All things that we ordained festival, turn from their office to black funeral*', says Lord Capulet after Juliet's feigned death (IV, v, 84–85). Similarly, when Juliet visits the priest to confess her sins ('*go to shrift*', II, v, 66), this becomes the occasion for her secret marriage, which would have been regarded as a sin against the rules of society and was indeed treated in this way in Shakespeare's source material (the poem by Arthur Brooke, cf. p. 15).

In terms of setting, the play pairs the intimate domestic world of the Capulet household with the formal public world ruled by the Prince. The conflict in the play – the fight for the lovers to be united despite the feud between the families – is illustrated by a variety of oppositions in the language (cf. p. 84) such as antitheses and oxymorons. Equally, there are contrasts in the dramatic mood of the play – the tragedy of the noble characters is constantly set in juxtaposition with the comic dialogue of the servants. This can seem shockingly inappropriate, as for example in Act IV, Scene 5, when the musicians make jokes immediately after the discovery of Juliet's seemingly dead body and the grief of her parents.

Love / Hate

'*Here's much to do with hate, but more with love*' says Romeo (I, i, 168), setting out the central theme of the play. '*My only love sprung from my only hate!*' cries Juliet (I, v, 137), when she discovers that Romeo, with whom she has fallen in love, is a Montague, the family that her family has been feuding with for many years. By the end of the play, the interplay of love and hate will have destroyed the two lovers and devastated their families; as the Prince tells their fathers: '*See, what a scourge is laid upon your hate, that heaven finds means to kill your joys with love.*' (V, iii, 292–293).

Love is discussed throughout the play. In the first three acts there are over one hundred references to love. Not only do the lovers themselves talk about love; many of the other principal characters also argue about it. The central love affair of Romeo and Juliet is played out against the backdrop of the two extremes of love: **courtly love**, which is always unhappy because it is never returned, and **bawdy sexuality**, which is purely physical.

Juliet has no idea what love is at the beginning of the play; she is thirteen years old, and our first view of her is of a dutiful daughter who is prepared to accept any man chosen by her parents (I, iii, 99–101). She learns about love when she meets Romeo, and her feelings for him are immediate and passionate. Within a few moments of meeting him, she is willing to give up her family if he will love her: '*be but sworn my love, and I'll no longer be a Capulet*' (II, ii, 35–36). This warmth evokes an equal response from Romeo who offers to be '*new baptised*' (II, ii, 50). He, too, will give up his name for love of her. Their names, associated with dispute and enmity, have immediately become '*hateful*' in the light of their affection for each other. '*My name, dear saint, is hateful to myself, because it is an enemy to thee*', says Romeo (II, ii, 55–56). This expression of passionate love, which aims at bringing the two lovers together, is in strong contrast to the courtly love expressed previously by Romeo in his unrequited feelings for Rosaline.

Courtly love, which was celebrated in poetry, particularly that of Petrarch (cf. p.16), was a form of love in which the man idealizes the woman. It is based on the view that human love is an elevated, almost spiritual experience. It is significant that we never see Rosaline, who remains the idealized object of Romeo's first passion. Shakespeare does not suggest that this form of courtly love is ennobling, but rather a form of sickness: it makes Romeo miserable, it upsets his parents and causes his friends to make fun of him. In Act II, Scene 3, Friar Laurence suggests that this kind of infatuation is learned and not genuinely experienced; Shakespeare later mocked such false emotion and exaggerated language in plays such as *As You Like It*. The language which Romeo uses to express his feelings for Rosaline is reminiscent of courtly love poetry. Juliet criticizes Romeo's overstated speech as '*Conceit, more rich in matter than in words*' (II, vi, 30), after which his language changes: it becomes less elaborate and less contrived. And we feel that this is the language of 'real' love. Language is a means of communicating one's feelings, and Romeo must learn to use real language to communicate real love.

Courtly love, which is essentially unrequited, is spiritual; 'real' love, on the other hand, is also physical. Within moments of meeting Juliet, Romeo kisses her. As soon as Juliet is certain that Romeo does love her, she tells him in the plainest, most direct language, to tell her messenger '*tomorrow*' exactly '*where and what time*' he will marry her (II, ii, 143–146). Yet while this love may be passionate and grounded in a physical reality (as can be seen by Juliet's expectations of the marriage night in Act III, Scene 2, and the difficulty of the two lovers in parting in Act III, Scene 5), it is also contrasted with the **bawdy sexuality** of the Nurse and the servants, which is merely physical without any pretence of emotional feeling. There is a great deal of sexual humour in the play (which is often played down or cut in performance). Indeed the play opens with the Capulet servants threatening to rape the young female Montague servants. Sampson says he will '*thrust his [Montague's] maids to the wall*' (I, i, 16–17). He and Gregory make sexual jokes about everything, as does Juliet's Nurse.

The Nurse speaks in prose, with frequent digressions, in contrast to the poetry of the noble characters. She is seen to be relaxed in her attitude to sex and to her own body. In conversation with Lady Capulet and Juliet, she talks about breastfeeding Juliet and reminisces about her late husband. She frequently jokes about the future sexual pleasures that Juliet will experience after marriage: '*happy nights to happy days*'. (I, iii, 107).

The love of Romeo and Juliet is also contrasted with the **hatred** between the two families. The families are imprisoned by this hatred – almost literally, as the wall that Romeo climbs over protects the Capulets and keeps out the Montagues. Outside the walls, there is a danger of the two families meeting. Benvolio comments (III, i, 3) that it is a hot day, the Capulets are about and '*If we meet, we shall not scape a* *brawl*. The personification of this hatred is Tybalt. We are introduced to him (I, i, 64) as a man who tells Benvolio that he hates the word peace '*As I hate hell, all Montagues and thee*'. He is enraged that Capulet allows Romeo to stay at the feast in Act I, Scene 5, and his determination to fight and kill Romeo brings about his own death, Romeo's banishment and the tragic outcome of the play. The hatred between the two families and their long-standing feud are necessary in the play, not simply because they create the tension between the lovers and the world outside, but because without them, the lovers would simply be disobedient children. The feud, for Shakespeare, was necessary so that he could change the audience's view of the lovers from the Brooke poem, where their deaths are justified as an outcome of their actions.

Love and hatred, like good and evil, are shown in the play to be inextricably bound up together and this necessary opposition is illustrated in Friar Laurence's soliloquy (II, iii, 7–30), where he reflects on the fact that plants contain both good and bad, and therefore can be both beneficial and poisonous.

Fate / Free will

Belief in prophecies and the role of fate was as strong in England in the early 17th century as it had been throughout the Middle Ages. The stars were believed to have a role in influencing the destiny of individuals and nations. Particular days and hours of the day were thought to be controlled by specific planets: Monday, for example, was linked with the moon and phlegmatic behaviour (cf. the Four Humours, p. 12).

The Prologue calls Romeo and Juliet '*star-crossed lovers*'. But how much of the play can be seen as the working out of **fate and destiny**? The play is full of coincidences, such as the accidental meeting of Peter with Romeo and Mercutio (which allows them to find out about the feast at the Capulets'), the delay of Friar Laurence's letter reaching Romeo, and Friar Laurence himself being delayed in getting to the tomb. In Shakespeare's other tragedies, the essence of the tragedy comes from a fatal flaw within the central character, such as Othello's jealousy or Macbeth's ambition, but in this play much of the tragedy happens simply because of bad luck or '*sour misfortune*' (V, iii, 82). This is signalled throughout the play: Friar Laurence says that Romeo is '*wedded to calamity*' (III, iii, 3) and Romeo, who describes himself as '*fortune's fool*' (III, i, 135), says in his final speech before he dies that he is finally giving up the burden of his fate: '*the yoke of inauspicious stars*' (V, iii, 111). Many critics have questioned the play's status as a tragedy because they feel that bad luck is not a worthy tragic theme. They note how much of the action appears to be the result of chance. It is bad luck that Romeo, in trying to stop the fight, allows Tybalt to kill Mercutio; it is unfortunate that Juliet's wedding to Paris is brought forward by a day. Friar Laurence is thoughtless when he fails to tell Friar John that the letter to Romeo is important, but it is also just bad luck that Friar John is held up by the quarantine. It might also seem to be bad luck that Romeo does not recognize Paris in the tomb, and the worst luck of all is his suicide just moments before Juliet wakes up.

The play can be seen as the unfolding of **a series of unlikely coincidences** which, in the hands of a lesser playwright, could seem melodramatic rather than tragic. Does the play simply show the impossibility of trying to escape one's fate? Is it, as at least one critic has suggested, an example of the hopelessness – as in Greek tragedy – of trying to defy the gods? Certainly the play is filled with astrological associations – the days of the week, the time of the day. Romeo and Juliet both know they are defying fate in loving each other: '*Then love-devouring death do what he dare*', Romeo declares (II, vi, 7) before his marriage. And again a contemporary audience would have known that fate tends to accept such a challenge. However, they take the decision to act in defiance of fate and in the belief that their love is worth the price it carries. While the audience might hope for a happy ending, it is the deaths of Romeo and Juliet which bring an end to the feud between their families, the '*ancient grudge*'. Their choice in loving each other is finally what heals the wounds of the city.

The moment at which the fate of the lovers is fixed is when Mercutio dies. His curse '*A plague o' both your houses*' is repeated three times (III, i, 90, 98–99, 105), which to contemporary audiences would have strengthened its power. This is the turning point of the play, which up to that point could almost be played as a comedy. But now the deaths of Romeo and Juliet are inevitable and this inevitability is emphasized by Romeo. '*This day's black fate on more days doth depend;*

this but begets the woe others must end.' (III, i, 118–119). And as Juliet notes: '*What must be shall be*' (IV, i, 21).

Time

Today's audiences are accustomed to a realistic portrayal of time and will complain if they discover discrepancies in character, time or plot in their favourite soap operas, films, etc. Shakespeare's audience demanded no such realistic form of plot, nor of time. As you can see from the timeline (cf. p.74) the entire action of the play takes place over five days. It begins at 9 a.m. on Sunday morning and ends on Thursday evening. Within that short space of time, Romeo and Juliet meet, fall in love, are married, separated and reunited in death. Romeo's speech to Friar Laurence telling him about meeting Juliet ('*We met, we wooed and made exchange of vow*'; II, iii, 62) ends with him asking the Friar to marry them the same day. During the same four days, Mercutio and Tybalt are killed, Romeo is banished, flees to Mantua, and then returns, the Capulets host a feast, organize first a marriage and then a funeral. It is not surprising that some commentators have said that the entire action of *Romeo and Juliet* feels like a dream, where the action is frequently speeded up and events happen without any logic. It is worth noting that the speeded-up time was an element introduced by Shakespeare. In the original sources, the time frame was several months, not just a few days.

The action is indeed accelerated from the moment that Romeo and Juliet meet. It is as if their love has precipitated them into fast-moving action from which there is no escape. Juliet compares this to lightning and it worries her: '*It is too rash, too unadvised, too sudden*' (II, ii, 118). At the beginning of the play, Capulet suggests (I, ii, 10) that Paris should wait two years before marrying Juliet, as girls are frequently harmed by early marriage. By Act III, late on Monday evening, Capulet is suggesting that Juliet marry Paris the next day. When Paris tells Friar Laurence this, the Friar notes that it is very soon – '*the time is very short*' (IV, i, 1). Paris replies that this is what Capulet wishes and he himself is '*nothing slow to slack his haste*' (IV, i, 3). This haste is increased – with tragic results – on Tuesday afternoon, when Capulet decides to bring the wedding forward to Wednesday morning.

Acts	Day	Time	Event
Act One	Sunday	morning	Montague and Capulet servants fight. Benvolio talks to Romeo's parents and then to Romeo.
		noon	Capulet talks to Paris about marriage to Juliet.
		evening	Benvolio and Romeo discover that there will be a feast at the Capulets'.
		night	Lady Capulet asks Juliet about marrying Paris. Guests arrive for the feast. Romeo and Juliet meet and fall in love.
Act Two	Monday	dawn	Benvolio and Mercutio cannot find Romeo.
		early morning	Romeo and Juliet declare their love for each other.
		morning	Romeo goes to Friar Laurence and tells him he wishes to marry Juliet.
		midday	Nurse meets Romeo and receives instructions for his marriage to Juliet.
		early afternoon	Romeo and Juliet are married.
Act Three		afternoon	Tybalt kills Mercutio. Romeo kills Tybalt.
		evening	Romeo is banished. The Nurse tells Juliet about Tybalt's death and Romeo's banishment.

		late evening	Romeo despairs. The Nurse brings him news of Juliet. He is to go to Juliet.
		night	Capulet decides to marry Juliet to Paris on Thursday.
	Tuesday	morning	Romeo and Juliet wake up together and part. Juliet is told she must marry Paris. She refuses and goes to the Friar for advice.
Act Four		late morning	Paris meets Juliet. Friar Laurence tells her how she can avoid the marriage. Juliet agrees to marry Paris. The marriage is brought forward to Wednesday.
		night	Juliet takes the potion.
	Wednesday	dawn	Juliet appears to be dead. Her family mourn.
Act Five	Thursday	morning	Romeo in Mantua hears of Juliet's death, buys poison and sets off for Verona.
		evening	Friar Laurence discovers that his letter has not been delivered to Romeo.
		night	Paris and Romeo meet and fight at Juliet's tomb. Romeo kills Paris. Romeo drinks the poison and dies. Juliet wakes and stabs herself.
		dawn	The city learns what has happened. The two families end their feud.

Having stayed up all night, it is only just after 3 a.m. '*the second cock hath crowed, [...] 'tis three o'clock*' (IV, iv, 3–4) when Capulet demands that Juliet get up for her wedding. It seems he cannot wait for the union to take place: '*Hie, make haste, make haste. The bridegroom he is come already. Make haste, I say*' (IV, iv, 26–28).

Whereas Romeo and Juliet live entirely in the present and near future, the older characters frequently talk about the past. The Nurse, for example, sees her life in terms of past events and church feast days: '*On Lammas-eve at night shall she be fourteen. That shall she, marry, I remember it well. 'Tis since the earthquake now eleven years*' (I, iii, 23–25). She constantly recalls the seasons, the weather, and where people were ('*My lord and you were then at Mantua*'; I, iii, 30). The Nurse's life has been formed by the past, and she frequently mentions past events that stand out for her. Capulet too reminisces about his past life (I, v, 31–39) and expresses his surprise at how quickly time has flown by.

The speed at which Romeo and Juliet's relationship develops is contrasted with the slow speed of others around them, especially their two confidants – the Nurse and the Friar. The Nurse's slowness in returning from Romeo and in delivering his message is not merely humorous, it also highlights the impatience of Juliet, who wants things to happen quickly. Confronted with Romeo's extreme joy at his marriage, Friar Laurence advises slowness in love: '*Too swift arrives as tardy as too slow*' (II, vi, 15), having previously warned him that is it wiser to be slow: '*they stumble that run fast*' (II, iii, 94). In the real world, Friar Laurence's advice might be worth listening to, but in the world of passion, Romeo's words '*I stand on sudden haste*' (II, iii, 93) are more convincing. Ironically, it is Friar Laurence's late arrival at Juliet's tomb that causes the death of the lovers; if he had been speedier, their lives might have been saved.

Youth / Age

While images of youth and old age can be found throughout *Romeo and Juliet*, the play is not a simplistic comparison of youthful impetuosity and wise maturity. The fighting between the families and the way in which Lord Capulet suddenly changes his mind and loses his temper are not signs of wisdom. Equally, the constancy of the two lovers cannot be equated with rash youth.

We do not know Romeo's age, but we are told many times how very young Juliet is. Shakespeare changed her age from that of his source material, making her almost fourteen instead of sixteen. Even before we meet her, Lord Capulet tells us her age and that she should wait two years before being married (I, ii, 9–11), while the question of whether she is ready for marriage is discussed at length. Romeo is also clearly young, which again we learn from conversations prior to his arrival on stage. His parents worry about him and his behaviour – he shuts himself up in his room all day and does not speak to anyone. This is not far removed from today's image of the typical teenager. The reason that Shakespeare made his protagonists so young might be so that they would be free of the burden of the feud between the two families. But this is also a play about adolescent love, and the youth of the two protagonists makes their passion and their mutual commitment all the more believable.

The old age of those around the lovers serves to illustrate how young and vulnerable they are. The first mention of Capulet, by Montague, refers to their old age: *'men so old as we'* (I, ii, 3). When Capulet calls for his sword, his wife suggests that he would do better with a crutch (I, i, 68–69). Capulet frequently talks about how different he is from when he was young. He reminisces with his cousin about his past exploits: *'I have seen the day that …'* (I, v, 20–21), but notes that such times are no more: *''tis gone, 'tis gone, 'tis gone'* (I, v, 23).

Old age is also seen in relation to its proximity to death. Juliet, when complaining how slow the Nurse is in returning from Romeo, notes that many old people behave as if they were already dead, *'Unwieldy, slow, heavy and pale as lead'* (II, v, 17). The irony of this is that it is the young (Romeo, Juliet, Mercutio, Tybalt, Paris) who die in this play, leaving the old to mourn. Two youngsters, Mercutio and Tybalt, end their lives early, due to their youthful impetuosity. Both of them are hot-headed young men, unable to think through the consequences of their actions. They only understand the need to put themselves forward and defend their pride. Only the peaceful, sensible Benvolio survives.

Masculinity/ Femininity

The ideas of masculine and feminine in this play are frequently characterized in terms of appropriate and inappropriate behaviour. Both Romeo and Juliet are criticized by others (and on occasions by themselves) when they stray from what is seen to be the correct conduct for their sex.

Romeo is first seen as the romantic lover, in the tradition of courtly love poetry, but there are indications that he is excessive in the way that he has adopted this role. His parents worry about his behaviour and his friends make fun of him. He is weak when a hero should be strong, while Juliet is strong and determined, where a woman 'should' be submissive and obedient. '*Thy beauty hath made me effeminate*', says Romeo (III, i, 113) when his love for a Capulet prevents him from fighting Tybalt, and he is ashamed. This shame echoes Mercutio's disgust that Romeo would not respond to Tybalt's challenge. Romeo shows none of the traditional heroic virtues of boldness and courage. He reacts to Juliet's suggestion of marriage, rather than proposing it himself, and after he has killed Tybalt, he is '*fearful*' (frightened). He weeps and is accused by the Friar of looking like a man but behaving like a woman: '*Unseemly woman in a seeming man*' (III, iii, 112), while the Nurse tells him to '*stand, and you be a man*' (III, iii, 88). At the end of the play, he kills himself for love, thus literally acting out the images of courtly love – that love is a disease, that a man dies for love. The association of Romeo with 'romantic' is achieved in his death.

Other variations on the theme of masculinity and femininity are introduced in the opening scene of the play in the sexual wordplay of the servants. Women are always available for sex, says Sampson because they are '*the weaker vessels*' (I, i, 14). But Juliet journeys through the action of the play from the dutiful daughter to the 'headstrong' girl who disobeys her father (III, v). From the innocent girl who has hardly dared think of marriage, she becomes a girl who, having fallen in love, will suggest marriage, be married in secret, and when betrayed by her closest confidante – the Nurse – risk her life and then choose to end it. The Friar may urge her to '*be strong*' (IV, i, 122), but to the audience she already is. Just as the images of the beautiful Juliet as light and the sun are reminiscent of the images used to praise Queen Elizabeth I, so the strength and masculinity of her character reminds us of Shakespeare's monarch who said of herself in 1588, when addressing the troops about to fight against the Spanish Armada: 'I know I have the body of a weak and feeble woman; but I have the heart and stomach of a king'.

Rosaline, who is never seen and is the embodiment of the courtly love image of the unattainable virgin, is determined to remain single and chaste. In Elizabethan England, this opportunity was in reality rare for women. Marriage was the only option, as there were no longer any convents in which single women could enjoy and wield power, as Henry VIII had destroyed the monasteries. Yet the image of a woman intent on remaining a virgin (i.e. keeping herself free from a husband, to whom she would in law belong) is one of strength, and is perhaps another reference to the 'Virgin Queen', who resisted marriage throughout her reign.

When Capulet plays 'the housewife', becoming involved in organizing the food for the wedding, he is rebuked by the Nurse as a '*cot-quean*' (IV, iv, 6), a term for a man who does women's work. He is acting out of character for a man. Similarly acting out of character, it is Lady Capulet who, after Tybalt's death, asks the Prince for justice and demands Romeo's life. The roles of masculinity and femininity are never taken for granted in this play and their reversals add to the complexity and interest of the characters.

▶▶▶ Language and Style

Different forms of speech

Romeo and Juliet is notable for its many juxtapositions of different forms of language. Comic sexual innuendo alternates with love poetry; joking with sadness; poetry (rhymed and unrhymed) with sections of prose. In Elizabethan drama, this mixture was not unusual. Comic and low-status characters generally spoke in prose and talked about matters of the day in colloquial language that would be familiar to the audience, while nobles and high-status characters spoke in verse. In *Romeo and Juliet*, some of the most emotional moments are expressed in the form of sonnets (see below) and for audiences of the period there would have been nothing strange in this.

Prose

Ironically, for modern audiences the prose sections are usually more difficult to understand than the verse sections. This is due to the fact that there is a lot of humour, especially word play, in the prose sections. In Elizabethan England, a person of nobility was judged by the quickness of their wit, and word play was one way of demonstrating a person's wit. Mercutio is the master of word play, yet his puns are hard to understand today because the meaning of the words has changed in English. The word '*goose*', for example, no longer means a prostitute as well as a bird (II, iv, 67–77), so the joking of Mercutio and Romeo falls flat for modern audiences. For this reason it is probably more important for you just to get the gist of the prose sections. For example, the first part of Act I, Scene 1 sets the scene of two households feuding and touches on the brutishness of sex without emotion; Act II, Scene 4 shows the audience that Romeo's new love has made him revert to his true witty fun-loving self, '*Now art thou sociable, now art thou Romeo*' (II, iv, 83); and we also learn that Tybalt is not a good swordsman, as he cares more about style than skill. While normally high-status characters speak in verse, the banter between Romeo and Mercutio in Act IV, Scene 4 is entirely in prose, perhaps because the scene is a comic interlude between scenes of high drama.

Strangely enough, Mercutio's death is also in prose. On the one hand, this serves to demonstrate the differing roles of Mercutio and Romeo. Mercutio's main role is as a light-hearted jester who mocks Romeo's feelings of love, so his dying speech cannot have the elevated status given to the death speech of Romeo, which is in verse. However, despite being in prose, Mercutio's final speech has tremendous energy and pathos, especially in the final sentences: '*No, 'tis not so deep as a well, nor so wide as a church-door; but 'tis enough, 'twill serve: ask for me tomorrow, and you shall find me a grave man. [...] Why the devil came you between us? I was hurt under your arm.*' (III, i, 95–102). Yet Mercutio's death is in many ways sordid: it is the result of a feud between two families (neither of which he really belongs to), of a provocation he made, and of a nasty piece of swordsmanship by Tybalt. A meandering prose speech is more appropriate than verse to mark his death.

Poetry

In the 1590s Shakespeare was a celebrated poet rather than a famous playwright, and *Romeo and Juliet* shows us something of the development of his poetic writing.

Shakespeare wrote in **iambic pentameters**, which contain five unstressed syllables alternating with five stressed syllables:

'*He jésts at scárs that néver félt a wóund.*' (II, ii, 1)

When used over several lines, this form of verse is called **blank verse**, which is considered the closest verse form to English speech. Previous dramatists had made every line adhere to the strict iambic pentameter form, with each line ending being **end-stopped** (i.e. punctuation, rhyming or the sense of the line made the actor pause at the end of each line). A good example is Friar Laurence's monologue in Act II, Scene 3, where each line ends with a rhyme:

FRIAR LAURENCE: *Young son, it argues a distempered head*
                       So soon to bid good morrow to thy bed.
                       Care keeps his watch in every old man's eye,
                       And where care lodges, sleep will never lie.
                       (II, iii, 33–36)

Shakespeare, like other dramatists, varied his lines. In *Romeo and Juliet* there are many examples where the meaning of a line runs into the following line (**enjambement**). A good example is Juliet's speech:

JULIET: *Dost thou love me? I know thou wilt say 'Ay',*
           And I will take thy word; yet if thou swear'st,
           Thou mayst prove false. **At lover's perjuries**
           They say Jove laughs. *[...]*
           (II, ii, 90–93).

Here each line flows on into the next, and the strict iambic pattern of unstressed followed by stressed syllables has been given up. The lines sound freer and are easier to speak. So while it is useful to know that the iambic pentameter is the basis of Shakespeare's drama, it is important to know that Shakespeare never used the form in a slavish manner.

There is a contrast in *Romeo and Juliet* between **courtly love poetry**, which was very popular in Shakespeare's day, and simpler, more truly felt poetry. Shakespeare often mocked pretension in his plays (see Mercutio's attack on the fashionable style of Tybalt's fencing; II, iv, 19–35) and his characters often use exaggerated and artificial verse when they are insincere or not true to their feelings. Friar Laurence tells Romeo that Rosaline knew he was insincere because of the way he spoke about his love: '*Thy love did read by rote, that could not spell*' (II, iii, 88). Juliet repeatedly tries to prevent Romeo from launching into a rehearsed expression of love. When he begins: '*Lady, by yonder blessed moon that tips with silver all these fruit-tree tops*' (II, ii, 107–108), Juliet stops him: '*O swear not by the moon*', to which he replies, '*What shall I swear by?*' and she answers '*Do not swear at all*'. His elaborate protestations of love worry her and make her begin to feel that their love may only be momentary, like lightning (II, ii, 119–120). She continues to criticize his use of such language just before their marriage: '*Conceit, more rich in matter than in words, brags of his substance, not of ornament*' (II, vi, 30–31). True love, she says, does not need to be described.

Mercutio also makes fun of courtly love poetry and its convention of naming the parts of a lady and praising them individually. Hoping to annoy Romeo into revealing himself, he begins: '*I conjure thee by*

Rosaline's bright eyes, by her high forehead and her scarlet lip, by her fine foot, straight leg and quivering thigh' (II, i, 17–19), and then continues with his punning and sexual innuendo.

When Shakespeare wants the audience to believe in the expression of his characters, he uses a more direct form of poetry, which avoids the use of clichés and formulaic love phrases, and which is also easier for the modern audience to understand:

JULIET:	*What o'clock tomorrow*
	Shall I send to thee?
ROMEO:	*At the hour of nine.*
JULIET:	*I will not fail: 'Tis twenty years till then.*
	I have forgot why I did call thee back.
ROMEO:	*Let me stand here till thou remember it.*
	(II, ii, 167–171)

Shakespeare also uses the **sonnet**, a very popular form of love poetry in the 1590s, three times in the play: the Prologue, the Prologue to Act II and at the key moment in the play – the first meeting of Romeo and Juliet. The sonnet is a sequence of 14 lines with a fixed pattern of rhymes (*abab, cdcd, efef, gg*) that sets out a proposition, which is then developed with a conclusion in the final two lines. A sonnet is normally a poem addressed to a lover, so Shakespeare's use of the sonnet in a play is unusual: the Chorus is given two sonnets (both of which discuss the action of the play), while the third one is spoken jointly by Romeo and Juliet (one of the few shared sonnets in the English language). In the sonnet the *b* and *d* rhymes are the same, which emphasizes the kiss which concludes the sonnet. For more discussion of this sonnet, see p. 28.

		rhyme
ROMEO:	*If I profane with my unworthiest hand*	a
	This holy shrine, the gentle sin is this.	b
	My lips, two blushing pilgrims, ready stand	a
	To smooth that rough touch with a tender kiss.	b
JULIET:	*Good pilgrim, you do wrong your hand too much,*	c
	Which mannerly devotion shows in this;	d
	For saints have hands that pilgrims' hands do touch,	c
	And palm to palm is holy palmers' kiss.	d

ROMEO:	*Have not saints lips, and holy palmers too?*	e
JULIET:	*Ay, pilgrim, lips that they must use in prayer.*	f
ROMEO:	*O, then, dear saint, let lips do what hands do:*	e
	They pray; grant thou, lest faith turn to despair.	f
JULIET:	*Saints do not move, though grant for prayers' sake.*	g
ROMEO:	*Then move not, while my prayer's effect I take.*	g

Style

Irony

Romeo and Juliet has many examples both of tragic irony and dramatic irony. **Tragic irony** occurs when an image is used which foreshadows future action. Thus the frequent use of the word poison in the play, such as when Romeo compares love to a '*choking gall*' (I, i, 187) is tragic irony because it is poison that kills Romeo at the end of the play. Similarly, when Romeo says of Mercutio that '*He jests at scars that never felt a wound*' (II, ii, 1) it is ironic, since Mercutio will soon die of his wounds.

Dramatic irony is a device whereby the audience knows more than the characters on stage. An example is the scene between Juliet and her mother after Tybalt has died (III, v), when the audience knows that Juliet is talking about Romeo, but Lady Capulet thinks she is talking about Tybalt. A similar convention is used when Juliet meets Paris (IV, i), and when Friar Laurence talks about Juliet after her apparent death (IV, v), as he and the audience know she is merely unconscious, but everyone else believes her to dead. Perhaps the greatest dramatic irony is when Romeo describes Juliet as still looking alive: '*beauty's ensign yet is crimson in thy lips and in thy cheeks, and death's pale flag is not advanced there.*' (V, iii, 94–96), without, of course, knowing that she is indeed alive.

Antithesis

This is a play about opposition and conflict: characters, events and settings are all placed in opposition to each other. Shakespeare develops the theme of opposition with the frequent use of verbal antithesis, where words themselves are placed in opposition: '*The grey-eyed morn smiles on the frowning night'* (II, iii, 1). Morning is the opposite of night, as are smiles of frowns. The conflict of the play is thus enhanced by its language. The most common groups of antithesis in the play are to do with love and hate: *'Here's much to do with hate, but more with love. Why, then, O brawling love! O loving hate!'* (I, i, 168–169); light and dark: *'More light and light; more dark and dark our woes!'* (III, v, 36); and good and evil: *'For nought so vile that on the earth doth live but to the earth some special good doth give.'* (II, iii, 17); while in the Prologue the tragic theme of the play is brought to our attention: *'death-marked love'*.

Antithesis is one of the techniques of rhetoric. All educated young men in Elizabethan England would have studied rhetoric at school and learned how to repeat the same point using different words. The Prince frequently employs this technique: *'Rebellious subjects, enemies to peace, profaners of this neighbour-stained steel'* (I, i, 74–75). Perhaps more than any other play by Shakespeare, *Romeo and Juliet* propagates antithesis as a philosophy. In the Prologue alone the Chorus informs us that the lovers issued from *'fatal loins'* (so even within conception death is foreseen). Furthermore contrasts are drawn between *'ancient'* and *'new'*, *'civil'* and *'unclean'*, *'parents'* and *'children'*. The Friar in his monologue (II, iii, 7–30) explains in detail how *'two such opposed kings encamp them still in man as well as herbs, grace and rude will'*; life is, in other words, a delicate balance of opposing qualities.

A particular form of antithesis is the **oxymoron**, which links together two apparently contradictory words (usually adjective + noun) such as *'loving hate'*. There are many examples of this in the play, for example in one of the most-quoted lines: *'Parting is such sweet sorrow'* (II, ii, 184). When Romeo first appears, he is suffering from unrequited love. He pairs *'heavy lightness'*, *'serious vanity'*, a *'feather of lead'*, *'bright smoke'*, *'cold fire'*, *'sick health'*, and *'still-waking sleep'* (I, i, 171–174). Juliet also uses this form after Tybalt's death when she accuses Romeo of looking angelic but being a monster, *'the opposite to what thou justly seem'st'* and calls him a *'beautiful tyrant! Fiend angelical! Dove-feathered raven! Wolvish-ravening lamb!'* and *'A damned saint, an honourable villain'* (III, ii, 75–79). Oxymorons express the confusion in the mind of the speaker who feels two distinct or opposing emotions.

Personification

Personification is a stylistic device by which abstract ideas are turned into people and given human attributes. Love and death are the abstract concepts that are most personified in the play. As the play is a tragic love story, this will probably come as no surprise. Love is often personified as the blind angel-like 'amor' with a bow and arrow: *'Alas, that love, whose view is muffled still, should, without eyes, see pathways to his will!'* (I, i, 164–165), *'With love's light wings did I o'erperch these walls'* (II, ii, 66) and *'If love be blind, love cannot hit the mark'* (II, i, 33).

Death is personified frequently in the play, and the word 'death' in fact occurs more often than 'love'. The Prologue introduces the image of death when it refers to the lovers as *'death-marked'*. Death is described as the destroyer of love, who actually competes as a lover for Juliet. Romeo challenges Death at the moment of his marriage *'Then love-devouring death do what he dare; it is enough I may but call her mine'* (II, vi, 7–8). When Romeo sees Juliet's body in the tomb, he says *'unsubstantial Death is amorous'* (V, iii, 103), an image that her father has already developed: *'Death is my son-in-law, Death is my heir, my daughter he hath wedded.'* (IV, v, 38–39). Romeo also personifies the tomb which has devoured Juliet: *'Thou detestable maw, thou womb of death, gorged with the dearest morsel of the earth'* (V, iii, 45–46).

Imagery
Light /dark

One of the most powerful aspects of *Romeo and Juliet*, and what sets Shakespeare apart from other playwrights, is his use of imagery. The most dominant image in the play is light. It appears in a variety of ways, as light itself, as the sun, the moon, the stars, lightning, fire, lanterns, etc. Juliet is presented in terms of light from the moment that Romeo sees her: *'O, she doth teach the torches to burn bright! It seems she hangs upon the cheek of night like a rich jewel in an Ethiop's ear'* (I, v, 43–45). When he stands below her window, he compares her with the sun: *'What light through yonder window breaks? It is the east, and Juliet is the sun.'* (II, ii, 2–3), later expanding this image, saying that *'The brightness of her cheek would shame those stars, as daylight doth a lamp'* (19–20). This image continues up to her death: *'For here lies Juliet, and her beauty makes this vault a feasting presence full of light'* (V, iii, 85–86).

Juliet also makes use of the imagery of light, she (ironically) wishes that after her death, Romeo would become a cluster of stars that would '*make the face of heaven so fine that all the world will be in love with night*' (III, ii, 23–24). Thus the brightness of the love affair is verbally constructed to shine out and dazzle the audience.

Light and dark, the sun and moon are also used antithetically, with one balanced against the other, thereby emphasizing the conflicts in the play. Light is not only a image which is used in a positive sense; light represents day when Romeo could be discovered and killed – both in the balcony scene and after he spends the night with Juliet. Juliet at this point dreads the day: '*More light and light; more dark and dark our woes*' (III, v, 36) as she had also longed for the '*love-performing night*' and wanted the sun to set and '*bring in cloudy night immediately*' (III, ii, 5 and 4).

Birds

Images in the play often come in clusters, frequently making antithetical use of opposites. There are a great many birds mentioned in the play, as well as images of wings and flight. Benvolio suggests that if Romeo goes to the Capulets' banquet, he will see so many beautiful women he will think that Rosaline is a crow, compared with so many swans. But the bird Romeo finds is Juliet, whom he compares to a dove among crows '*So shows a snowy dove trooping with crows*' (I, v, 47). The bird imagery works on many levels. The discussion by Romeo and Juliet (III, v) as to which bird is singing, the lark, which represents the day, or the nightingale, which represents the night, is also a warning, as mistaking the bird could lead to discovery and death.

When Romeo first arrives under Juliet's window, he says that he flew over the orchard walls with '*love's light wings*' (II, ii, 66). However, this imagery of love freeing the couple from imprisonment is counterbalanced by the willingness of the couple to learn and be trained by the other. Juliet compares Romeo to a hawk, a '*tassel-gentle*' (II, ii, 159) and Romeo calls her his '*nyas*' (II, ii, 167), a young hawk, in response. Later, Juliet uses the images of falconry to compare her first love-making to the expectations of a young hawk that is kept hooded and is ready for its first hunt: '*Hood my unmanned blood, bating in my cheeks, with thy black mantle*' (III, ii, 14–15). Romeo wishes he were

Juliet's captive bird on a string (II, ii, 182). The lovers use the imagery of falconry to establish their loyalty to each other. But while Romeo may have taken Mercutio's advice to '*borrow Cupid's wings*' so that he can '*soar with them above a common bound*', both he and Juliet prefer the imagery of trained and loyal birds tied to a master to explain their love for each other.

Religion

While Romeo and Juliet cannot consummate their love until it has been sanctioned in marriage by a priest – anything else would have been unthinkable in Elizabethan England – it is love itself that is given religious significance. Juliet recognizes this when she tells Romeo to swear by himself '*Which is the god of my idolatry, and I'll believe thee*' (II, ii, 114–115). When they first meet they use religious imagery extensively: Romeo compares Juliet to a shrine and uses the image of the pilgrim, hands together in prayer, to touch Juliet. Juliet uses conventional religious practice – going to visit the priest to make confession or saying her prayers '*I have need of many orisons*' (IV, iii, 3) to conceal her real actions. Thus there is a constant opposition of traditional religious practice against which the image of love as a kind of religion is played out. In choosing to kill themselves, Romeo and Juliet act against the principles of the Church. The kiss that they both demand as they die is a continuation of the heretical kiss they exchanged when they first met. And while it is the feud between the families that is cited as the reason for the death of the young couple, religion also plays its part. The Prince recognizes this: '*See, what a scourge is laid upon your hate, that heaven finds means to kill your joys with love*' (V, iii, 292–293).

Glossary of Literary Terms ◄◄◄

Act: The major division of a drama; it is usually subdivided into scenes. Most of Shakespeare's plays are divided into five acts.

Aside: Words spoken by a character in a play which the audience, but not the other characters, can hear. An aside reveals the thoughts and intentions of the character, and may often contrast with what he or she says to the other characters. There are very few asides in *Romeo and Juliet*. Romeo, for example, is described as speaking 'aside' when Juliet appears at her window in Act II, Scene 2; Juliet speaks aside when her mother insults Romeo (III, v, 81). Occasionally an actor will speak aside while others are on stage, e.g. Tybalt (I, v, 53–58); while this is not marked as an aside, it is clear that Capulet does not hear his lines. An aside is similar to a soliloquy, except that other characters are present on stage, and an aside may consist of little more than one line.

Blank verse: Unrhymed verse consisting of five iambic feet (an iamb consists of an unstressed syllable followed by a stressed syllable). It is also called the iambic pentameter. It is often used by Shakespeare as it is close to the rhythmic patterns of English speech. However, blank verse very rarely follows the iambic metre closely.

> *I drew to part them. In the instant came*
> *The fiery Tybalt, with his sword prepared*   (I, i, 101–102)

Comic relief: The use of humour to lighten the mood of a serious or tragic story. The technique is very common in Shakespeare's works. In *Romeo and Juliet* one can see the comic relief as reflecting on the theme of love, as much of the humour is sexual, indicating that love-making may be reduced to a merely physical act.

Enjambement (also '**run-on line**'): In a poem or in blank verse, a sentence that runs on from one line to the next without a pause.

> *In fáir / Veró /na, whére / we láy / our scéne* (Prologue, 2)

Prose: Prose is all writing that is not in verse. While Shakespeare usually uses verse forms like blank verse, he also employs prose in various scenes in *Romeo and Juliet*. Prose is often used by the characters with low status (e.g. Sampson and Gregory in Act I, Scene 1) or when the characters are using lewd language (e.g. Mercutio, Benvolio and Romeo in Act II, Scene 4).

Rhyming couplets: Two successive rhyming lines. In *Romeo and Juliet* Shakespeare uses rhyming couplets to indicate that a scene is over (as there were no curtains or scene changes in those days):

> *I'll go along, no such sight to be **shown**,*
> *But to rejoice in splendour of mine **own**.* (I, ii, 102–103)

There are other examples of rhyming couplets, e.g. Lady Capulet's description of what to look for in a man and Friar Laurence's speech about good and evil (II, iii, 1–30). The rhyming couplets underline the fact that these lines contain interesting information.

Scene: A subdivision of an act of a play, usually consisting of unity of time, place and action

Soliloquy: A speech delivered by a character alone on stage. It is used to reveal a character's thoughts, feelings or motives to the audience. It allows the audience to learn more about the character than would be possible if only action and dialogue were presented. Juliet's speech (II, v, 1–16) is a good example of a soliloquy, as it shows her passion, eagerness and impetuosity.

Sonnet: A poem with 14 lines with a fixed pattern of rhymes (*abab*, *cdcd*, *efef*, *gg*) that sets out a proposition, which is then developed and they concluded in the final two lines. Sonnets were normally addressed to a lover, so Shakespeare's use of sonnets in a play is unusual. Moreover, the Chorus is given two sonnets (both of which discuss the action of the play), while the third one is spoken jointly by Romeo and Juliet; their sharing of the lines of the sonnets is a strong indication that the two are meant for each other.

Stage directions: A playwright's notes in the text of a play which give information about how the drama is to be performed. Stage directions may deal with any of the following: setting, scenery, characters' appearances and manner of speaking, and entrances and exits by characters. We do not know if Shakespeare wrote the stage directions to his plays.

Coping with Exam Papers

Generally, tasks on texts, whether they are fictional or non-fictional, fall into three categories: 1) **comprehension**, 2) **analysis** and 3) writing a **composition** or a **personal comment**.

1. Comprehension

All comprehension tasks aim at finding out whether you have **understood** the play. Usually you are given an extract and are asked to locate it within the framework of the whole play. You must select the relevant events which lead up to the extract and which take place afterwards. When answering comprehension questions you should refrain from stating your own opinion, unless expressly asked to do so.

2. Analysis

Analysis tasks go beyond a simple understanding of the text. You may be asked to deal with the whole play or to deal with the selected extract in detail. Analysis questions often concern language and imagery, characters, or the way the plot is structured. Here again, you should avoid giving your own opinion. Be careful not to retell the story: you really need to analyse what is happening on a more abstract level, e.g. don't just say what a character does, but explain why he or she does it, or find an adjective to describe the character, etc.

3. Evaluation

This area covers a wide range of different tasks. Indeed you may be offered a choice of two tasks.

You may be asked to write a **composition** or a **comment**, which often require you to show that you have understood what the intention of the play is. Tasks often deal with a general interpretation of the play so make sure your ideas are plausible and well argued. This means that your ideas have to be in line with the play and that you must always be able to prove what you say by referring to the story. Never just make a supposition and leave it at that.

You may be asked to write a 'personal comment', which means you are obliged to give your own opinion, so make sure you base it on informed judgement, for which you need a thorough knowledge not just of the play but also of the way it is constructed, so avoid making statements which you cannot prove.

Often you will be given the choice of doing a 'creative task'. Although at first this may seem easy, you should only choose to do a creative task if you have practised enough beforehand and your teacher seems happy with your work in this area. Creative tasks can involve:

- reflection on other characters or events: this can often be in the form of a diary entry;
- filling in the gaps: here you might be asked to fill in what the reader does not learn directly from the text. This can often be in the form of a letter, an extra scene or an additional piece of dialogue.

Whatever kind of creative tasks are set, you must remember to stay within the context of *Romeo and Juliet*. This means that you must not simply fantasize but look, for example, at the way a certain character behaves.

Operative Words

Regardless of which category of tasks you are dealing with, it is extremely important to read the task carefully and look for the operative words, which tell you exactly what is required of you. Here is a list of common operative words, in alphabetical order. (They are not necessarily confined to comprehension, analysis or composition)

Analyse ...: an analysis is a detailed examination of, for example, an important topic, or one or more of the characters, so you must deal carefully with all the relevant aspects.

Assess ...: here, you must consider in a balanced way the points for and against something.

Comment on ...: here you are allowed to give your personal opinion on, for example, the way characters behave, but you must always give evidence from the play to support it.

Compare ...: you must highlight similarities and differences, most frequently between characters and events. A similar kind of task is:

Contrast ...: here, however, you must concentrate on the differences.

Describe ...: in this kind of task you must show what something (e.g. setting) or somebody (one or more of the characters) is like by giving a detailed account. Be careful not to forget any relevant details and choose examples from the text to illustrate the points you have made.

Discuss …: if you are asked to discuss a particular aspect of the play (e.g. the characters and how they interact), you should examine the issue from all sides before you state your personal opinion.

Evaluate …: here, you must form an opinion after carefully considering and presenting the advantages and disadvantages of a particular situation or course of action.

Examine …: this is another way of asking you to **analyse** something.

Explain …: this kind of task involves giving reasons for the action, characters' motives or how the specific use of certain techniques like the use of imagery produce a certain effect.

Characterize / Describe somebody's character …: here you should describe the specific features of, most often, one or more characters, by looking at how they speak.

Illustrate …: here, you have to make something clear by choosing relevant examples. Read the task carefully to find out whether you have to concentrate on the given passage or whether you may, or have to, refer to the whole play.

Interpret …: here you should deal with both form and content and how they work together to create meaning.

Justify …: here you must argue why something should be done or some decision taken or why some conclusion was made.

Outline …: an outline is a general account of something. In other words in your outline you can retell the major events of a story, or give a brief description of a character, which includes only the very relevant elements only and omits all details.

Point out …: here, you must find and explain certain aspects of the text.

Present …: here, you are expected to write something down in your words.

State …: here, you are expected to specify clearly whatever is required. You may be required to state the main features of or development of something.

Summarize …: a summary is more precise than an outline. When writing a summary you should select the key points and ideas etc. and structure them. As in an outline you should not go into detail or give examples. You might, for example, be asked to summarize a dialogue or argument, or the events of the whole play or an extract.

General points to remember – or how to impress the examiner:

- You are not writing for yourself, but you are addressing the examiner(s) who will mark your work. Examiners are not mind-readers, so you must express yourself as clearly as possible.

- Always **collect and organize your ideas** before you start writing. In this way the examiner will be able to follow you more easily.

- When writing a composition or a personal comment, remember three simple steps: say what you are going to say – say it – sum up what you have said. Doing this will make your text more convincing.

- When you are dealing with literature you should always use the **simple present tense** when discussing characters and action.

- Structure your work by using **'connectives'** to link your ideas, so that the examiner can follow the presentation of your arguments. Otherwise he or she gets the impression that you are 'rambling'. You should be able to find a list of connectives in your coursebook.

- Likewise, **avoid all forms of repetition**, unless you want to return to a point you made earlier on. In this case you should use expressions like 'as I have already pointed out …'

- You can always impress the examiner by using suitable **quotes**, but they should only be used to **underline** a point you have already made or are going to make, and not instead of making a point – otherwise the examiner will think you are simply copying from the text or that you are unable to express yourself correctly. Always put your quotations in inverted commas. If you are allowed to use the book, you should also refer to the page and line of the quote.

- Usually the test paper will tell you how many words you have to write for each section of the test. If you have time after re-reading and checking your paper for coherence, mistakes, etc., try and count your words, as you may have marks deducted for writing too little or too much.

Written Test

At some stage while reading *Romeo and Juliet* in class, you will have to do a written test. What the test looks like depends on how much of the play you have read, and to a certain extent on the *Bundesland* you are in. Here you are offered one written test.

Declarations of Love

90 JULIET:	Dost thou love me? I know thou wilt say 'Ay',
	And I will take thy word: yet if thou swear'st,
	Thou mayst prove false. At lovers' perjuries
	They say Jove laughs. O gentle Romeo,
	If thou dost love, pronounce it faithfully:
95	Or if thou think'st I am too quickly won,
	I'll frown and be perverse and say thee nay,
	So thou wilt woo. But else, not for the world.
	In truth, fair Montague, I am too fond,
	And therefore thou mayst think my behaviour light.
100	But trust me, gentleman, I'll prove more true
	Than those that have more coying to be strange.
	I should have been more strange, I must confess,
	But that thou overheard'st, ere I was ware,
	My true love's passion. Therefore pardon me,
105	And not impute this yielding to light love,
	Which the dark night hath so discovered.
ROMEO:	Lady, by yonder blessed moon I swear
	That tips with silver all these fruit-tree tops –
JULIET:	O, swear not by the moon, the inconstant moon,
110	That monthly changes in her circled orb,
	Lest that thy love prove likewise variable.
ROMEO:	What shall I swear by?
JULIET:	Do not swear at all;
	Or, if thou wilt, swear by thy gracious self,
	Which is the god of my idolatry,
115	And I'll believe thee.
ROMEO:	If my heart's dear love –

JULIET: Well, do not swear. Although I joy in thee,
                   I have no joy of this contract tonight:
                   It is too rash, too unadvised, too sudden;
                   Too like the lightning, which doth cease to be

120   Ere one can say 'It lightens'. Sweet, good night!
                   This bud of love, by summer's ripening breath,
                   May prove a beauteous flower when next we meet.
                   Good night, good night! As sweet repose and rest
                   Come to thy heart as that within my breast!

91 **swear'st**: swear (that you love me)

93 **Jove**: Jupiter

97 **but else, not for the world**: but otherwise, I would rather not do so for anything at all

98 **fond**: infatuated; foolish; tender-hearted

99 **light**: morally loose, improper

100 **true**: constant, faithful

101 **coying to be strange**: pretending in a cunning way to be different from what they are

102 **strange**: distant, reserved

103 **but that**: if it had not been for the fact that

103 **ware**: aware

105 **impute**: unterstellen

105 **yielding**: Nachgeben

106 **which**: refers to 'yielding'

106 **discovered**: revealed

109 **inconstant**: changing

110 **circled orb**: sphere in which the moon circles the earth

114 **idolatry**: Vergötterung; Götzenverehrung

116 **joy**: rejoice

117 **contract**: exchange of lover's vows

118 **unadvised**: done without careful consideration

121 **bud**: Knospe

122 **beauteous**: beautiful

Tasks:

1 Briefly explain the situation Juliet and Romeo find themselves in, and say what their dialogue is about.

2 Analyse the dialogue with special focus on the language and what it reveals to you about the two characters, their attitudes towards love and their differing gender roles.

3 Either

a) Pick out various lines that you think are interesting for the future development of the story. Write a comment about them.
Or

b) Imagine you were in the audience watching *Romeo and Juliet*. Invent a dialogue in the interval in which you talk to a friend specifically about this dialogue within the framework of the play.

Dealing with the test

What is written below are not answers, but hints and things for you to think about so that you can write your own answer.

1

This dialogue is the second meeting between Romeo and Juliet. He has climbed during the night into the Capulet garden in the hope of seeing her. She comes to her window and expresses her love for him without knowing he is listening. He speaks up and this exchange follows shortly later.

The dialogue is about how they should tell each other that they love each other. It is important as we see how both characters, on finding their true love, change also their way of behaving and speaking.

Writing your answer

When you write your answer, you need to give a convincing opening sentence that relates to the question. Something along these lines: 'This dialogue takes place at the beginning of Act II when Romeo and Juliet meet in private for the first time.'

You are asked to 'explain the situation Romeo and Juliet find themselves in'. Here you need to mention what has happened beforehand, but you should avoid writing a summary of everything that has happened so far, but just mention those facts and events relevant to understanding this scene. You could mention the following: Romeo has been depressed as he was in love with Rosaline, who did not return his feelings; Juliet had until now been the obedient and dutiful daughter willing to fulfil her parents' expectations concerning a marriage to Paris; when they both attend a party at the Capulet house, in which he intends to observe Rosaline and in which Juliet is to be observed by Paris, they see each other and fall in love; however, they learn that they belong to feuding households.

You are also asked to explain what the dialogue 'is about'. Here you need to say that Juliet is trying to find out whether Romeo really loves her, or whether he is just using romantic language to woo her.

When answering this question, you should avoid quoting and listing any images, etc. from the dialogue. This answer should be written in your own words.

2

Particularly interesting is the difference between Romeo and Juliet's views of love. The audience in Act I was shown a young man who was unhappy in love, as his beloved did not return his love. He used flowery language to speak about love and his sadness. Now he has a real live woman in front of him, who seems willing to return his feelings. Yet he is unable to prevent himself from expressing his love in clichéd phrases. He swears by 'yonder blessed moon that tips with silver all these fruit-tree tops'. The reference to the moon is not very original, and the use of 'silver' reinforces the feeling that he likes 'rich' phrases. His knowledge of courtly love tells him he must swear his love by something valuable, but Juliet dismisses his need. He then says the phrase 'my heart's dear love', again using words that one would expect in a declaration of love.

Juliet, on the other hand, rejects his linguistic efforts, as she does not feel that courtly language is appropriate for real love. As a woman, she is very aware of her role in matters of love. Should she go too far, she stands to lose her reputation. In much of the play, there are sexual innuendos about men and their use of women sexually, and about the diseases that can be transmitted by sex. Juliet fears Romeo may think she is promiscuous ('light') by her sudden declaration, but she assures him that she would rather be direct and honest than play the role of the coy woman. And she requires from Romeo a declaration that shows him to be serious. For this reason she keeps cutting him off when he is about to launch into a speech about his feelings of love.

What is surprising is the way Juliet shows herself to be a mature, determined woman. The audience had previously only experienced her as a young girl prepared to be married to a stranger. Here she reveals that she not only knows the rules of courting, but is aware of how precarious her position is. Moreover, it is she who is telling Romeo what to say and what not to say.

Writing your answer

Remember that 'analysis' is required, so avoid rewriting what is said in the dialogue. Style is always an important factor in analysing how an author achieves a particular effect. For this you will need vocabulary such as 'images', 'metaphors', 'metaphorical language'. Words reflecting the state of Juliet's and Romeo's mind like 'anxious', 'uncertain', 'worried', 'full of hope', 'loving', 'impetuous' and 'passionate' may be useful. You will also need to use words from the word field of love and passion: 'woo', 'court', 'declare your love'.

Your task is to link all these ideas together. You will find words and phrases like 'show', 'illustrate', 'demonstrate', 'seem', 'appear to be', 'probably' and 'possibly' will help.

Connectives (e.g. 'moreover', 'on the one hand …, on the other …') will also come in useful for making your text coherent.

An example might be: 'While, Romeo, on the one hand, uses courtly language to express his feelings, Juliet, on the other, continually requests him to avoid such language and to speak plainly.'

3

a) Here you should consider express your feelings concerning this speech in general. Possible things to consider might be: Is Juliet too 'rash'? Might this be a cause of the tragedy? Would it be better for both of them to follow their traditional gender roles? Is Romeo too immature to be a husband? Should one be worried by the mention of her love as being 'idolatry'? Does their love indeed turn into 'a beauteous flower'?

b) In the dialogue you should take everything you have said so far into account. You do not need to have an argumentative dialogue but can move from one idea to the other. You may also bring in aspects you have not mentioned in your other aspects, such as the use of imagery or antithesis (light and dark; lightening and night)

Writing your answer

Your style should be neutral if you are writing a comment. If you are writing the dialogue, you should situate the dialogue in the opening sentences, e.g. 'So, do you think this meeting leads necessarily to their deaths?'. The dialogue partners must react to the other's statements. The style should remain informal but should avoid slang (it is after all a Shakespeare performance).